Internet Projects for Primary

Finding Information

Michael Strachan and Frances Thomas

A & C BLACK

***The Authors**:* Michael Strachan and Frances Thomas are qualified teacher-trainers of Primary school teachers in the use of computers in schools.

Published 2001 by
A & C Black (Publishers) Limited
Alderman House
37 Soho Square
London W1D 3QZ

ISBN 0-7136-5703-0

Acknowledgements
This book was produced for A & C Black by
Bender Richardson White, Uxbridge.

Project Editor: Lionel Bender
Designer: Malcolm Smythe
Art Editor: Ben White
Illustrations: Jim Robins
Production: Kim Richardson

Teachers' Notes and Photocopiable Activities created by: Lucy Poddington

Cover illustration: Charlotte Hard

A CIP catalogue record for this book is available from the British Library.

CONTENTS

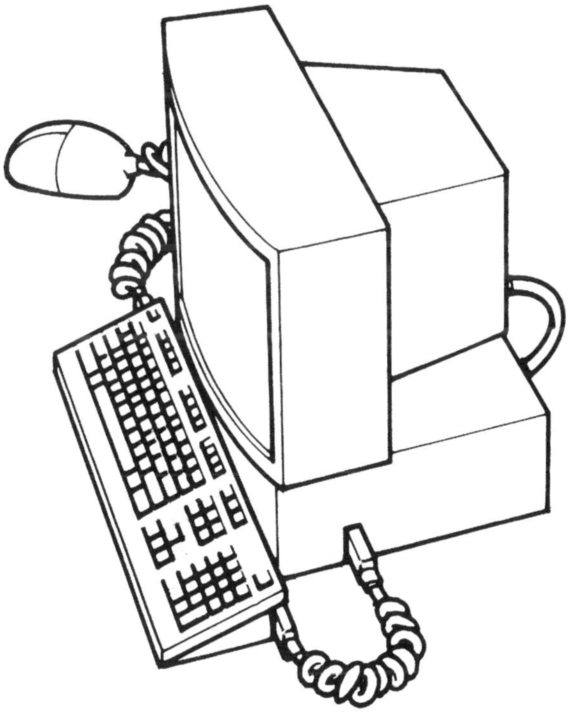

ABOUT THIS BOOK

This book is a practical guide for those working with children to help them to get on the Internet and search the World Wide Web for information. It has been written by teachers with the help of Literacy and ICT educational advisors. It is a resource to help both adults and children build up confidence and skills in Information and Communication Technology across the National Curriculum. Material is organised and explained in a practical way, using non-technical language. Where technical terms cannot be avoided, they are explained in the Glossary on pages 93–95.

If you are a Key Stage 2 classroom teacher, an ICT co-ordinator or newly qualified, this book will show you how to use the Internet to find information for your professional development, for research in lessons and for use in the classroom.

If you are a teacher with experience in ICT, then the practical projects in this book should be particularly useful. You will also find ideas to help you train and support less-experienced colleagues.

If you are a trainee teacher, you will find the practical classroom advice valuable as you build up your repertoire of teaching skills and expand your understanding.

If you are a parent who wants to take an active role helping your child through the maze of the Internet, then this book will help you support your child's teachers in promoting the best use of the Internet as a learning tool.

Finding Information aims to make sense of the Internet and show you how it can be an important part of teaching and learning. The book focuses on *Windows* PCs running *Internet Explorer* software but can be used with *Netscape Navigator* software and Apple Macintosh or Research Machines' computers.

BOOKS TO MAKE SENSE OF THE INTERNET

At first, trying to get into cyberspace can be daunting. There is a lot of jargon, and the technology keeps changing. The basics, however, are not that difficult to grasp. *Finding Information* is one of three ICT titles, produced by teachers for teachers, about making the best educational use of the Internet. Each title has more than 30 photocopiable activity sheets.

The other two titles are:

Using E-Mail Practical aspects of using e-mail to communicate with people and organisations around the world.

Creating A Web Site Clear instructions and illustrated examples explaining how to build and manage a web site.

Section 1: Introduction

The 'Introduction' contains background information about the Internet, how it works and how to make the best educational use of it. There is a brief history of its development along with a summary of the Government's requirements for planning purposes.

Section 2: Getting Online - The Basics

This section provides a step-by-step guide to getting online and exploring the Internet. There are diagrams, computer screen shots and a minimum of text. Many pages give practical hints and tips as well as curriculum guidance notes. The section includes features on browsing and focused searching, downloading text and images, and how to print out resources accessed on the Internet.

Section 3: Questions and Answers

This section answers some frequently asked questions, such as 'What can go wrong?' and addresses security issues. It also describes the hardware and software you will need to get online, and the basic computer skills you should develop.

Section 4: Photocopiable Projects

Photocopiable activity sheets provide teachers with activities for children to do in classroom groups of pupils or individually. These will help children to get the most out of Internet learning by offering focused tasks that encourage critical thinking.

At the start of the section are Teachers' Notes. These give ideas and suggestions for making the most of the activities.

Most of the activity sheets end with a challenge, called 'Next Step', which reinforces and extends the children's learning and provides the teacher with an opportunity for assessment. These more challenging activities might be appropriate for only a few children.

The activities cover a wide range of curriculum subjects and are pitched at different learning levels. Some can be carried out away from the computer. Others are designed to be completed by using the Internet. The activities can also be carried out at home.

Section 5: Recommended Web sites

This part of the book lists recommended web sites and links that teachers have found especially useful.

Section 6: At-a-Glance Guides

Finally there is a glossary and a computer skills checklist that can be photocopied and pinned up alongside computers.

SECTION 1:
INTRODUCTION

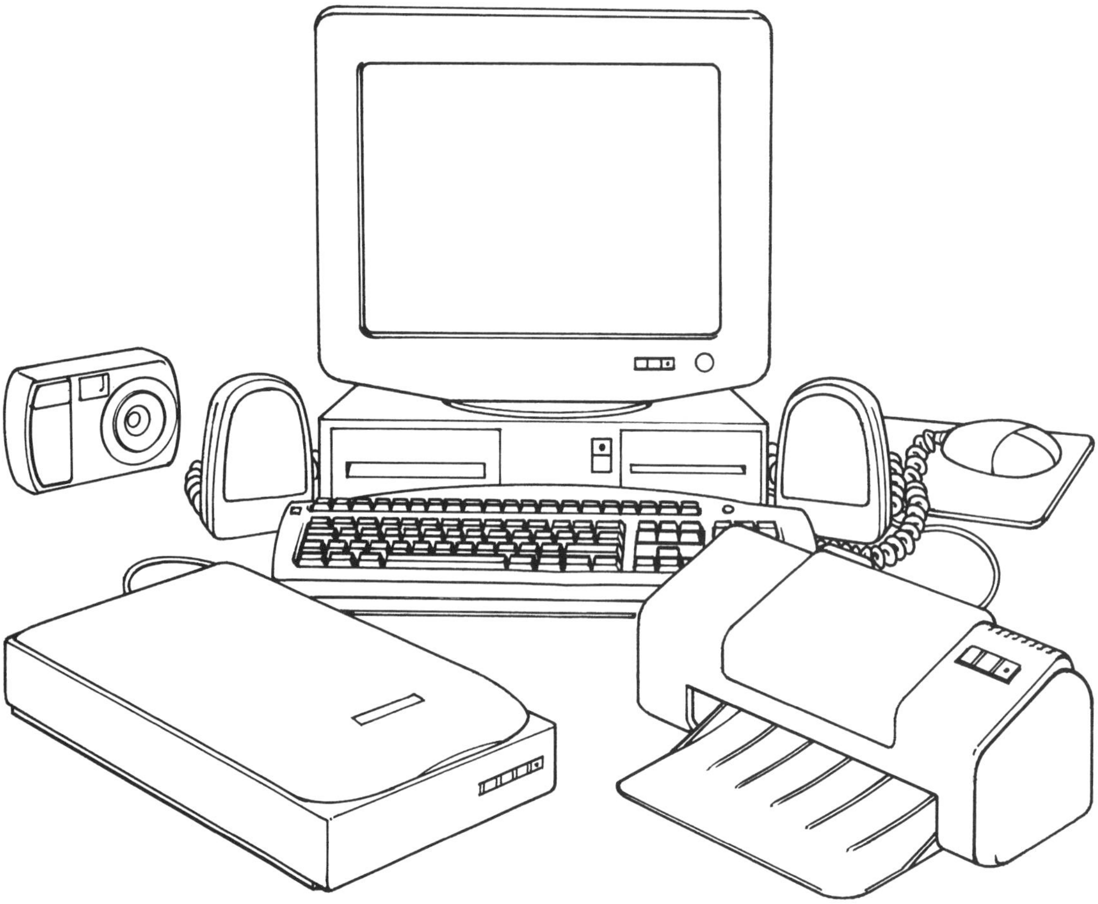

What is the Internet?

The Internet is simply a worldwide group of computers made up of lots of smaller groups called networks. All these networks are connected by special computers called servers, and can share information using telephone lines, cables, modems and radio. You can access the Internet by linking up your computer to one of the servers.

The huge collection of information available on the Internet is known as the World Wide Web. The information is stored at 'web sites', which are are created by individuals and organisations on their computers. A web site consists of a collection of 'web pages', each of which you can access on your computer screen. All you need to do to search for information – otherwise known as 'surfing the Internet' – is to call up your Internet server and key in the unique 'address' of the web site you want to explore.

One of the features that makes the Internet so exciting and an excellent educational tool is that the shared information includes not only text but also images, films, music, sounds and video. Another feature of the Internet is that the information can be transmitted and received anywhere, anytime, cheaply and quickly. Wherever you are, you can connect your computer into this vast network and access any of the resources 365 days of the year.

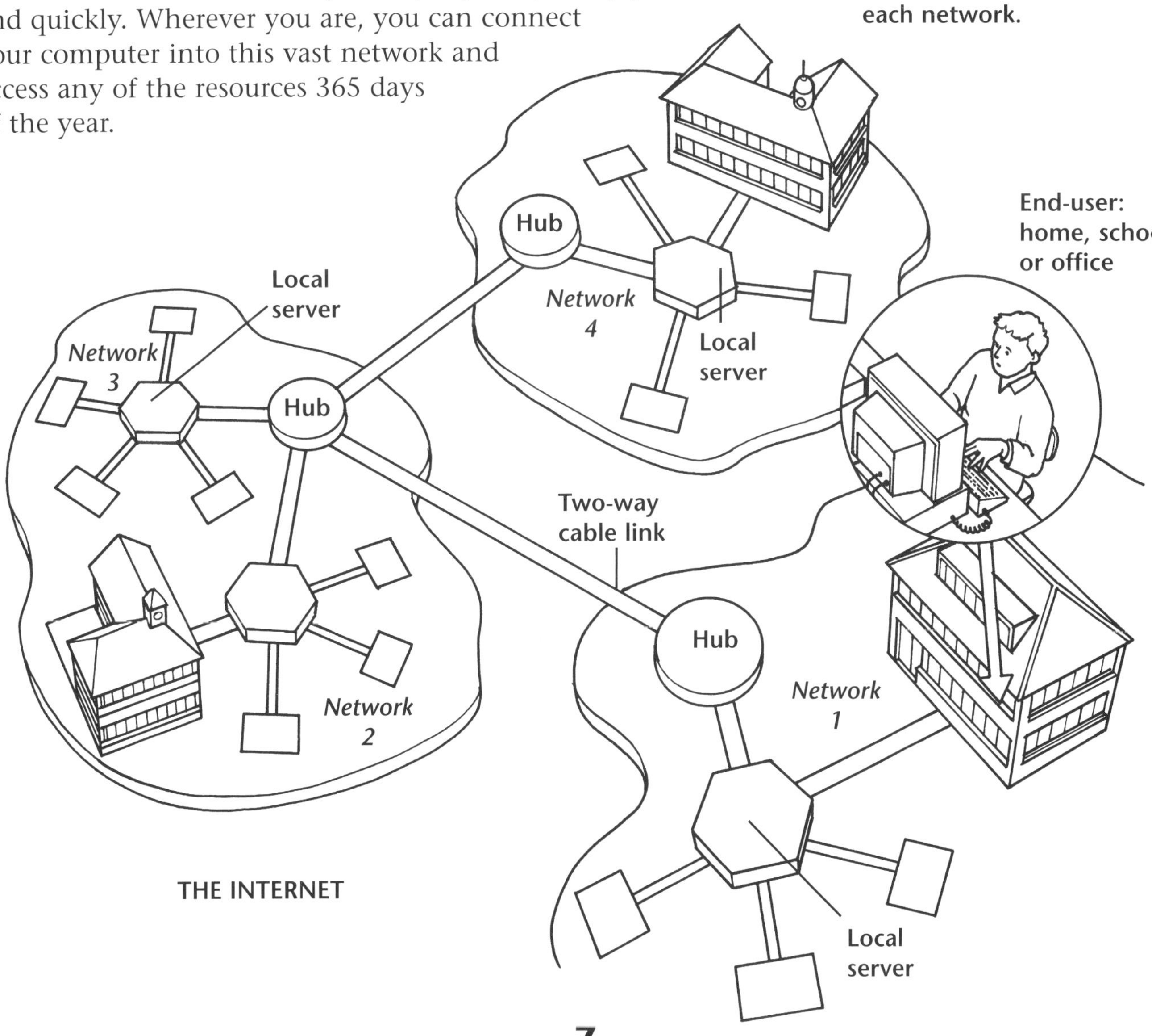

In this example, four computers are linked to a local server in each network.

THE INTERNET AND THE NATIONAL CURRICULUM

Using the Internet is part of Information and Communication Technology (ICT), which is a foundation subject in the National Curriculum. This means it is expected to be at the heart of the educational process and used wherever it is appropriate and helpful.

The Government has published its blueprint for the Internet and Education for the new millennium. It sees the World Wide Web as a 'mosaic of interconnected sites'. The web sites include:

- commercial content-providers
- academic sites with educational resources developed for the classroom
- web sites designed by schools.

By accessing these different types of sites, pupils and teachers will be able to work together to find and share information.

The statement of the National Curriculum Information and Communication Technology requirements for Key Stage 2 is shown opposite. Read this through to see how finding information on the Internet is fundamental to modern educational practice. The statements most relevant to using the Internet are underlined.

HINTS AND TIPS

Much of the curriculum information from the Department for Education and Employment (DfEE) and the Qualifications and Curriculum Authority (QCA) is already online.

You can visit the DfEE and QCA web sites at:

www.dfee.gov.uk

www.qca.org.uk

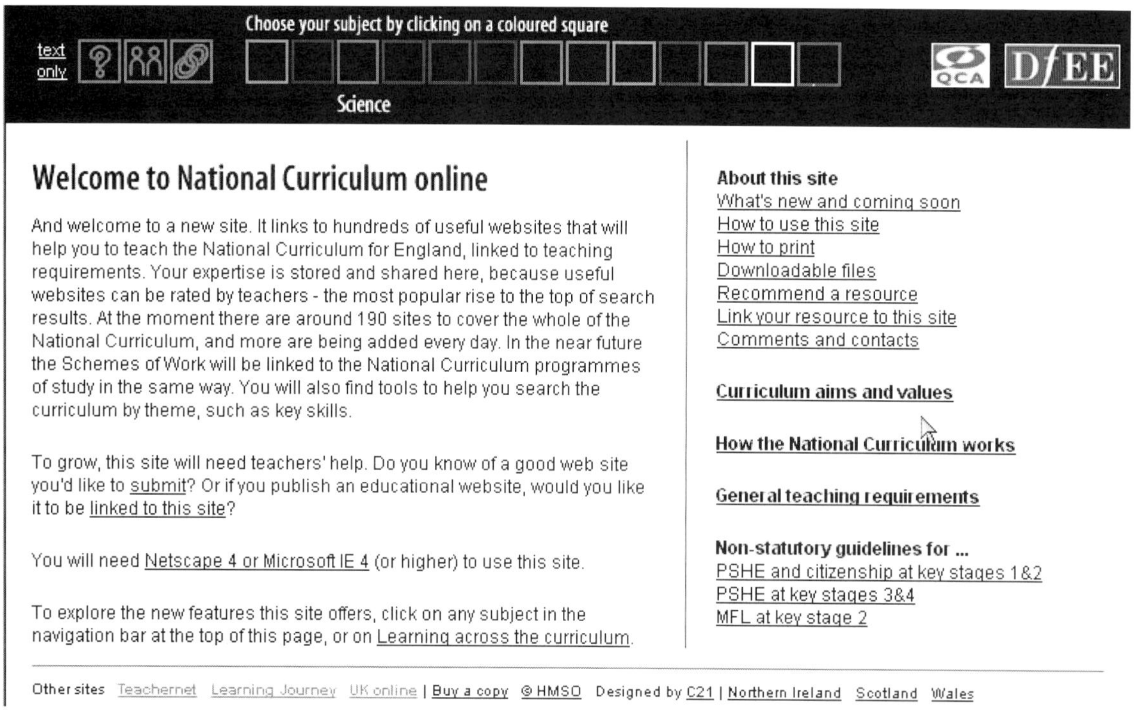
text only
Choose your subject by clicking on a coloured square
Science
QCA
DfEE

Welcome to National Curriculum online

And welcome to a new site. It links to hundreds of useful websites that will help you to teach the National Curriculum for England, linked to teaching requirements. Your expertise is stored and shared here, because useful websites can be rated by teachers - the most popular rise to the top of search results. At the moment there are around 190 sites to cover the whole of the National Curriculum, and more are being added every day. In the near future the Schemes of Work will be linked to the National Curriculum programmes of study in the same way. You will also find tools to help you search the curriculum by theme, such as key skills.

To grow, this site will need teachers' help. Do you know of a good web site you'd like to submit? Or if you publish an educational website, would you like it to be linked to this site?

You will need Netscape 4 or Microsoft IE 4 (or higher) to use this site.

To explore the new features this site offers, click on any subject in the navigation bar at the top of this page, or on Learning across the curriculum.

About this site
What's new and coming soon
How to use this site
How to print
Downloadable files
Recommend a resource
Link your resource to this site
Comments and contacts

Curriculum aims and values

How the National Curriculum works

General teaching requirements

Non-statutory guidelines for ...
PSHE and citizenship at key stages 1&2
PSHE at key stages 3&4
MFL at key stage 2

Other sites Teachernet Learning Journey UK online | Buy a copy © HMSO Designed by C21 | Northern Ireland Scotland Wales

From the National Curriculum:

'During Key Stage 2 pupils use a wider range of ICT tools and information sources to support their work in other subjects. They develop their research skills and decide what information is appropriate for their work. They begin to question the plausibility and quality of information. They learn how to amend their work and present it in a way that suits its audience.'

These requirements are divided into five areas:

1. Knowledge, skills and understanding
2. Developing ideas and making things happen
3. Exchanging and sharing information
4. Reviewing, modifying and evaluating work as it progresses
5. Breadth of study

1. Knowledge, skills and understanding

PUPILS SHOULD BE TAUGHT:

a to talk about what information they need and how they can find and use it (for example, searching the Internet or a CD-ROM, using printed material, asking people);

b how to prepare information for development using ICT, including selecting suitable sources, finding information, classifying it and checking it for accuracy (for example, finding information from books or newspapers, creating a class database, classifying by characteristics and purposes, checking the spelling of names is consistent);

c to interpret information, to check it is relevant and reasonable and to think about what might happen if there were any errors or omissions.

2. Developing ideas and making things happen

PUPILS SHOULD BE TAUGHT:

a how to develop and refine ideas by bringing together, organising and reorganising text, tables, images and sound as appropriate (for example, desktop publishing, multimedia presentations);

b how to create, test, improve and refine sequences of instructions to make things happen, and to monitor events and respond to them (for example, monitoring changes in temperature, detecting light levels and turning on a light);

c to use simulations and explore models in order to answer 'What if . . .?' questions, to investigate and evaluate the effect of changing values and to identify patterns and relationships (for example, simulation software, spreadsheet models).

From the National Curriculum (continued):

3. **Exchanging and sharing information**

PUPILS SHOULD BE TAUGHT:

- **a** how to share and exchange information in a variety of forms, including e-mail (for example, displays, posters, animations, musical compositions);
- **b** to be sensitive to the needs of the audience and think carefully about the content and quality when communicating information (for example, work for presentation to other pupils, writing for parents, publishing on the Internet).

4. **Reviewing, modifying and evaluating work as it progresses**

PUPILS SHOULD BE TAUGHT TO:

- **a** review what they and others have done, to help them develop their ideas;
- **b** describe and talk about the effectiveness of their work with ICT, comparing it with other methods and considering the effect it has on others (for example, the impact made by a desktop-published newsletter or poster);
- **c** talk about how they could improve future work.

5. **Breadth of study**

DURING THE KEY STAGE, PUPILS SHOULD BE TAUGHT THE KNOWLEDGE, SKILLS AND UNDERSTANDING THROUGH:

- **a** working with a range of information to consider its characteristics and purposes (for example, collecting factual data from the Internet and a class survey to compare the findings);
- **b** working with others to explore a variety of information sources and ICT tools (for example, searching the Internet for information about a different part of the world, designing textile patterns using graphics software, using ICT tools to capture and change sounds);
- **c** investigating and comparing the uses of ICT inside and outside school.

What Does the Internet Offer Teachers, Parents and Pupils?

The Internet links all of us to vast databases of information. It allows us to visit people, places and organisations all over the world via their web sites. It offers a rich and varied content for all curriculum areas and for pupils of every ability and interest.

Below is a list of some major categories of information on offer. The addresses of web sites related to each category are given in Section 5 of this book.

SEN Resources and Information

There are web sites that specialise in providing information and resources for parents and teachers of children with Special Educational Needs (SEN).

Curriculum Information and Updates

Schools and teachers can use the Internet as the first port of call when seeking information about the curriculum and classroom practice. In addition to DfEE web sites, there are a number of Virtual Teachers' Centres.

Information for Parents

Keeping up with what is going on in school is easier than ever. More informative web sites are coming online, some sponsored by the Government. The BBC provides excellent information.

Multimedia

The Internet has many web sites dedicated to providing multimedia resources of all kinds, including pictures, video and audio clips. Information from these sites can be integrated into children's projects.

Educational Games

There are also many sites that have educational games, tests and quizzes, designed specifically to encourage problem-solving or to test general knowledge.

Encyclopedias and Exam Revision Notes

Many well-known encyclopedias, dictionaries and other reference works are available online. Educational publishers provide teach-yourself lessons and revision courses. Colleges, libraries, students and teachers from all over the world are making their revision notes and essays available to anyone.

Books and Authors

Some sites have complete or abridged works, quotations or bibliographies of famous authors. You can use passages of famous texts for classroom activities. If your pupils are studying a particular author, try searching by that author's name. You may be surprised by how many sites you find dedicated to that author's life and works.

Question the Experts

If you and your pupils know where to go, you can find an expert on just about any subject. Increasingly, the educational content of the Internet is including real-time links to specialists and experts. That means that it is possible to ask an expert a question and receive an answer almost immediately.

Specialist Interests

Research institutions and government agencies have created web sites containing text, images, films and sounds for anybody to use. These resources can help bring curriculum subjects to life. For example, NASA provides images of planets, space vehicles and astronauts.

Virtual Museums and Galleries

One of the most exciting possibilities of the Internet is the availability of great works of art, music and scientific knowledge from museums all over the world. Many offer virtual reality tours. This means that your pupils can walk through art galleries or see a museum's collection which they may, otherwise, not be able to visit.

Using the Internet in the Classroom

It is important for schools to have up-to-date equipment and software so that children can access the resources offered by the Internet. Above all, it is important for teachers to develop their own computer skills, so that they can guide their pupils and help them to get the most out of the Internet. Also, as more children have access to computers at home, teachers need to be aware of what the Internet offers and how it is accessed.

Teaching New Skills

To use the Internet productively, pupils need to be taught good research skills at the outset. Once they learn to be focused, they will save time and effort throughout their school careers and be able to gather more useful information. Getting information by a roundabout route can be fun, and browsing can be rewarding, but knowing where you are going before you start out is more efficient.

Children learn to make sense of their world from talking and interacting with other children and with adults rather than from computers. It is in the warmth and excitement of a well-organised Primary classroom or in a supportive home that children can try out ideas and begin to put the facts into some kind of structure.

Computers and the Internet have a crucial role to play in displaying the world – past, present and future – to young learners, but this experience needs to be guided and supported.

Classroom Resources

Of course, there are times when books, paper and pencils or tape recorders are more appropriate tools to use in a particular activity. Also, it can be more practical to assess a child's progress by checking his or her written work than it is to review the child's efforts on the computer.

Children may need paper and pencils in preparation for searching for information on the Internet, and afterwards for writing up or illustrating their investigations. Many of the photocopiable activities in Section 4 of this book enable children to plan their layouts and record their results.

When working with children on computers, whether at school or home, it is also a good idea to have books, paper and pencils available for when the machine 'crashes' or you cannot get on to the Internet because the telephone lines are busy or broken.

Planning Lessons

Before venturing on to the Internet, you need to be comfortable with some basic computer 'household management'. You need:

- word-processing skills
- mouse and keyboard skills
- the ability to save, organise and manage files.

You will find a basic checklist of computer skills in Section 6. Work through this list and practise the skills until you are confident.

You will also need to plan your lessons in advance and to record their outcomes. Your school probably already has a documented system for recording details of planning, delivery, follow-up and assessment of curriculum activities. If not, then a simple form like the one shown below may be helpful. Whatever system you use, it should be quick and easy. It should cover the National Curriculum requirements, the classroom preparations, how the lesson/activity was delivered or carried out, what follow-up took place back in the classroom and a brief assessment of the process.

Currently, it may be too much work for your school to move this kind of documentation online, but the example shown here exists in the program Adobe *Acrobat* online format and could be used as the basis.

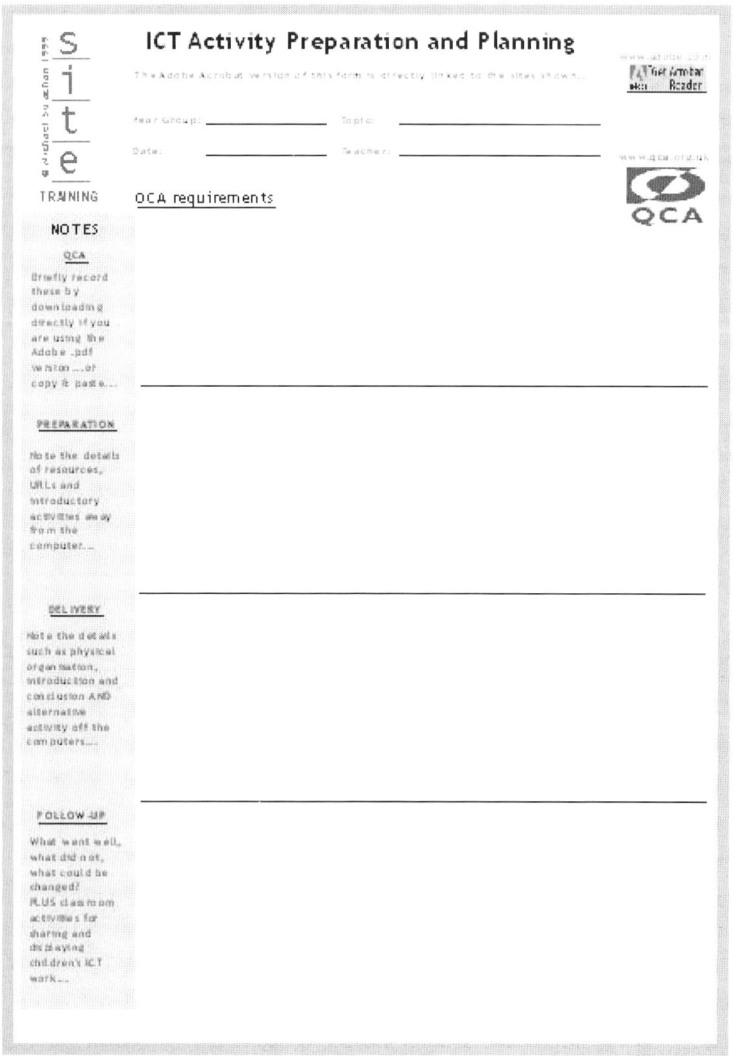

site TRAINING

ICT Activity Preparation and Planning

Year Group: ______ Topic: ______

Date: ______ Teacher: ______

QCA requirements

NOTES

QCA

Briefly record these by downloading directly if you are using the Adobe .pdf version ....or copy & paste...

PREPARATION

Note the details of resources, URLs and introductory activities away from the computer...

DELIVERY

Note the details such as physical organisation, introduction and conclusion AND alternative activity off the computers....

FOLLOW-UP

What went well, what did not, what could be changed? PLUS classroom activities for sharing and displaying children's ICT work...

QCA

Get Acrobat Reader

Adopting a Critical Approach

There is such a vast flow of information to be accessed on the Internet that it can be difficult to identify what is worthwhile. You can filter out some material by conducting your searches from a web site, such as the National Grid for Learning (NGfL) web site. This is a gateway, or portal, to many other educational sites. In Section 5 of this book, we have listed the NGfL web site address plus those of many other recommended sites.

Time is a major limiting factor when using computers in the classroom. One way to avoid wasting time searching for information on the Internet, is for children, parents and teachers to share their experiences of good and bad web sites. Make up your own lists of recommended sites and circulate this to your pupils and colleagues.

Following up Searches

There are numerous ways that you and your children can follow up research on the Internet. Here are some suggestions:

- Make and maintain a list or chart of search engines and particularly useful or interesting web sites used in your classroom, with notes about their suitability for particular subjects and topics.
- With children, compile lists of keywords under topic headings.
- Download and copy pictures/music/sound/video excerpts into suitable software such as *Powerpoint* or *Textease* to produce simple slide shows or project packs.
- Save, store or print simple information/pages for others to use in the projects.
- Compile topic books/news-sheets and so on, for other audiences.
- Collaboratively produce topic questionnaires for others to use. These can be for any subject.
- Groups can compile reports on selected aspects of a topic, for example Tudor food and drink, fashion, houses and homes.

Linking to the Internet

Most homes and many Primary schools are equipped with stand-alone computers, that is, computers that are not linked by cables to any other computer. Provided such a computer has a modem (it can be separate or built-in) and the appropriate software, it can be used to search for information on the Internet.

Some homes and an increasing number of schools are networked. This means that one machine acts as a server (host). The host computer is connected all the time to the Internet. It stores and relays the software and web site information to the other computers in the network. The diagram below shows the principles of a school computer network.

A SIMPLE CABLE NETWORK

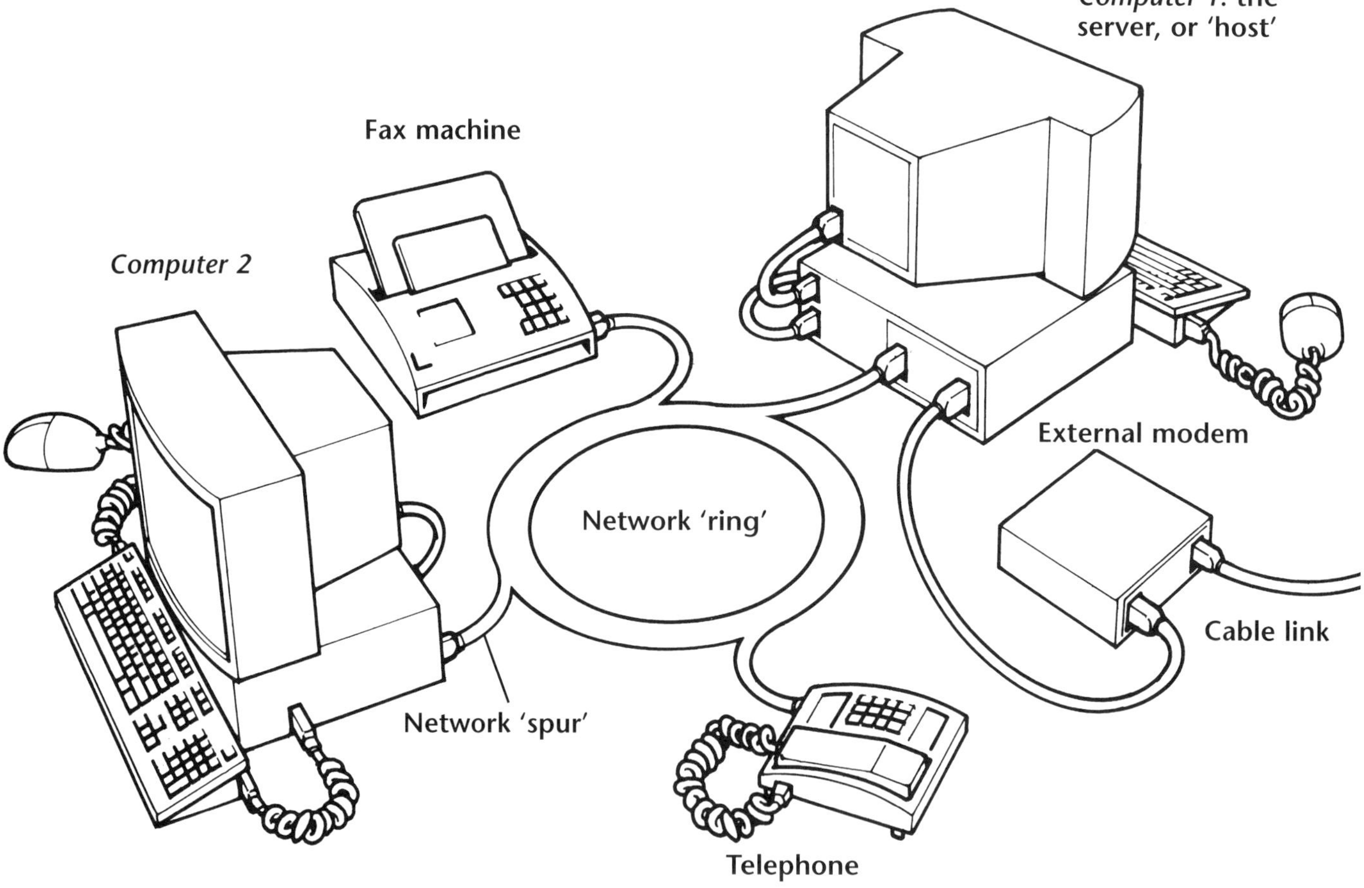

As teachers at school you will be linked to the Internet by an Internet Service Provider (ISP). This is a company that provides the school's Internet connection via a telephone line and probably also supplies the software needed to search the Internet and use e-mail.

When you switch on your computer and log in, you will be taken to the ISP home page (starting page), which will have a number of useful links set up for you. *Research Machines (RM)* is an educational online service provider – another is *Argosphere*. They connect your school to the Internet and also provide a range of content and resources, and incorporate a system to filter out dubious links and web sites.

Going it Alone

If you have not yet got your own computer, here are some guidelines to help you choose the ideal machine. First, you need to decide whether to buy a personal computer (PC) running *Windows* software, or an Apple Macintosh computer (usually shortened to just Apple Mac, Apple or Mac). It is best to have the same type of computer at home as you or your children use at school.

1 Talk to friends and colleagues who have recently bought machines and get their views, particularly on the help and support offered as part of the package. Then visit the computer stores and look at the demonstrations to compare the range of machines on offer. Take a knowledgeable friend with you.

2 Avoid the hype. Look for a PC or Mac with a modem and the largest hard disk you can afford. The hard disk is where you store programs and the files you create. It needs to be at least 4 Gigabytes (Gb) and preferably more.

3 You also need short-term memory power called random-access memory (RAM) – at least 64 Mb. You need at least 128 Mb RAM to deal with big images, video or DVD files.

4 An Internet Service Provider (ISP) should provide the affordable link on to the Internet. Networked schools will have been contracted with an ISP during purchase and installation. Individuals may find this already set up on the computer they buy. Find out about an ISP before committing yourself to using them.

5 The support contract and guarantee are crucial. Having someone who will visit your home in person to sort out problems is invaluable, whereas a telephone hotline may just cause further frustration. Make sure your support contract also covers the printer.

Hints and Tips

If you are buying your own equipment, make sure you have an on-site support contract.

Get at least a 17" monitor, for an easier display.

Choose a computer that has as much hard disk capacity (RAM) as you can afford.

Technical Notes

The processor is the microchip at the heart of any computer. The speed at which it processes information is measured in megahertz (MHz). The higher the number, the faster the computer goes. Your computer needs at least 600 MHz to give you fast access to the Internet.

An internal modem is the box that connects you to the Internet. The speed at which the modem connects you is measured in kilobytes per second (Kbps) – the faster the connection, the better.

6 A good laser or inkjet printer is important. Many deals now come with the printer bundled in. If you are choosing a printer separately, check how much the ink cartridges will cost to avoid too much ongoing expenditure, and find out how many pages per minute it prints to avoid unnecessary time-wasting.

7 Scanners and digital cameras are fun and, if they come as part of the package, you will certainly find many uses for them. For example, if you take pictures of your class on an educational visit, you can put the photographs straight on to the computer network. You can also scan postcards or other souvenirs of the trip.

A COMPUTER SYSTEM

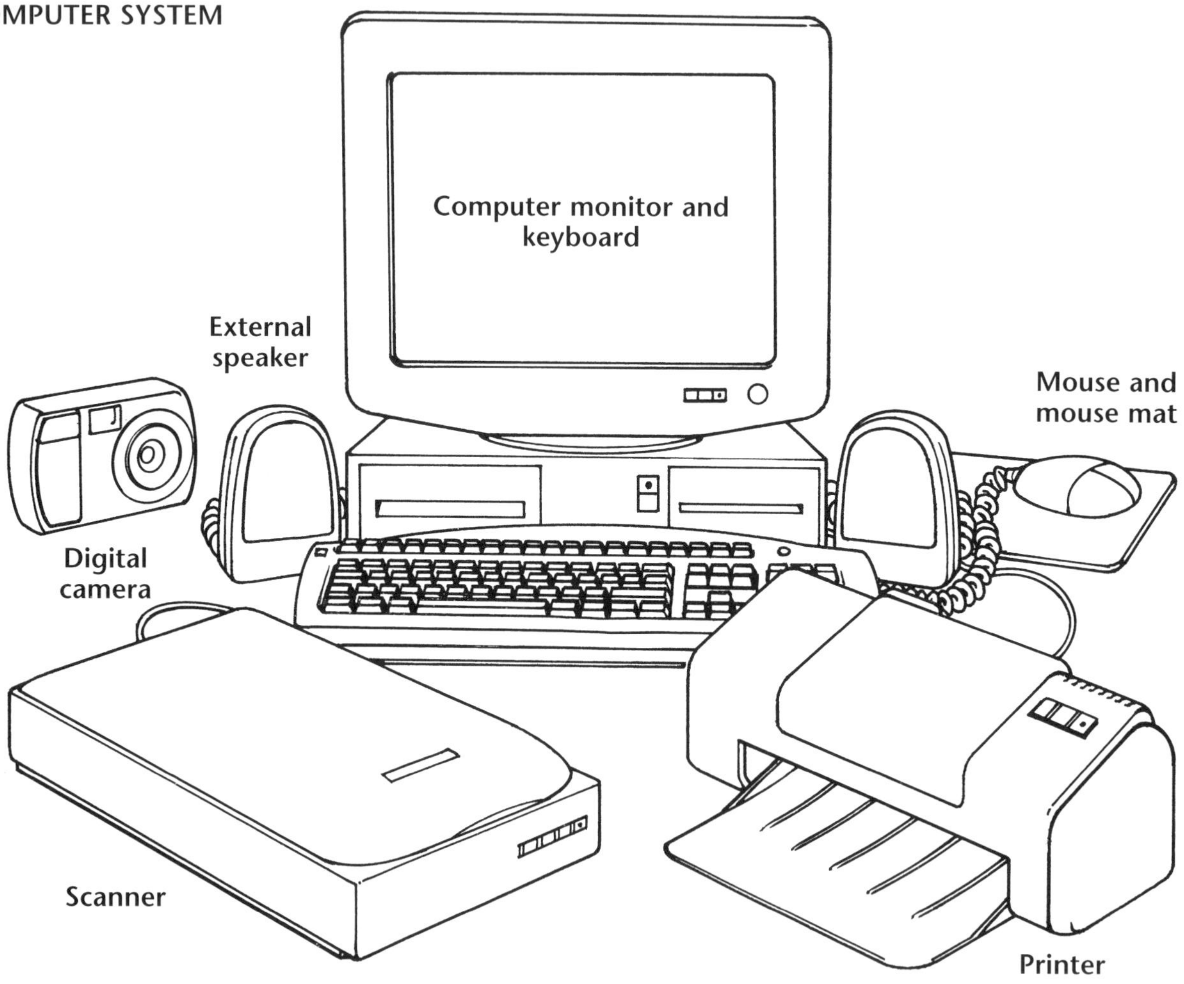

8 You will probably find it easier and cheaper to buy a complete 'package', like the one shown here, rather than combine individual components. Look for special offers in computer shops or advertised in the national press.

Choosing an ISP to Use at Home

If you are setting up a computer system at home, in order to browse the Internet and send e-mail, you will need to sign up with your own choice of ISP. Online services such as *America OnLine* (*AOL*) and *BT Internet* connect you to the Internet, and so do other smaller ISP companies.

The online services provide plenty of their own content, including chatrooms and messenger services. Most of the smaller ISP companies provide very little original content. You just use their services to venture out on to the Web and find what interests you.

You need to consider costs as well as content. Even connection services that appear to be free may have hidden costs. Here are some questions to consider when choosing an ISP:

- Is there a monthly fee or subscription?
- Is there an affordable annual charge?
- Are there extra charges for being online?
- Does the company provide a CD-ROM with pre-configured connection software for your computer?
- Is there readily available, free telephone support?

Once you have considered these factors, get on the Internet and get started!

A Brief History of the Internet

Like so many ground-breaking technologies, computers and the Internet were conceived in time of war. During World War II, the Enigma code-breakers at Bletchley Park in England never imagined that, in their lifetimes, the computer systems they developed to solve numerical codes would shrink from their house-sized machines to tiny accessories.

Worldwide Networks

The Cold War of the 1960s was the driving force that saw smaller desktop computers becoming common in universities and research institutions in the United States. The idea of a global network of computers was proposed in 1962, and by 1965 a Massachusetts computer was connected successfully to one in California over the telephone line.

It made military sense for the US Government, its key agencies, university departments, research companies and others to be connected electronically by adaptable networks. It was thought that, in the event of attack, enough of the system of government would survive and, hopefully, important messages could still be transmitted and vital records protected. This system, known as ARPANET (Air Raid Precaution Advanced Network), was brought online in 1969. In the following years many other universities and government contractors joined in the new network.

Everyday Computers

It was in 1989 that the initiative returned to Europe. Desktop computers were becoming more powerful and now had a host of new user-friendly features, such as a graphical interface (a display screen with clickable pictures), a mouse for moving around a pointer on the screen, and more storage memory. Instead of typing in lines of complicated code, even a newcomer could point a mouse to an on-screen picture called an icon and click a button to send instructions or save data for later retrieval.

Data-Swapping

Throughout this period, scientists were at the forefront of computer development. At the research laboratories of CERN (European Organisation for Nuclear Research), the foundations for the Internet were being laid. All of the projects, researchers and computers at CERN needed a way of swapping information freely, so that new developments would be accessible to all.

As computers became part of school and home life, devising software for them grew into a multi-million dollar industry. The Internet, however, was still just a network of smaller networks. There was no systematic way of connecting all the bits of information that were flying around with all their destinations.

Scientist Tim Berners-Lee and others at CERN established that computers needed to be speaking the same language; otherwise electronic communication would be chaos. The language they devised is now called TCP/IP (Transmission Control Protocol, or Internet Protocol) and it ensures that data sent from one computer to another is dealt with in a special way.

All data, whether text or images, is broken down into 'packets'. Each packet is tagged with information about its point of origin and its destination. When the packets arrive, they are assembled in the right place and in the right order. All this is done in fractions of a second and no one really notices anything unless it goes seriously wrong!

The CERN scientists also established that every information site needed a specific address; the data should be laid out in pages, and there should be links between those pages. Once every web site and web page had a URL (Universal Resource Locator) or web address, cross-linking them was possible. The 'hypertext' concept was born. Hypertext within pages was highlighted in colour or underlined. When you moved the computer mouse cursor over this text, it changed from a pointer to a hand symbol. Clicking the mouse button took you directly to a new web site or web page.

Hypertext also meant that it was possible to link 'hot spots' (specific locations on pages) with each other. Two page locations on completely separate web sites could be linked.

A WEB SITE

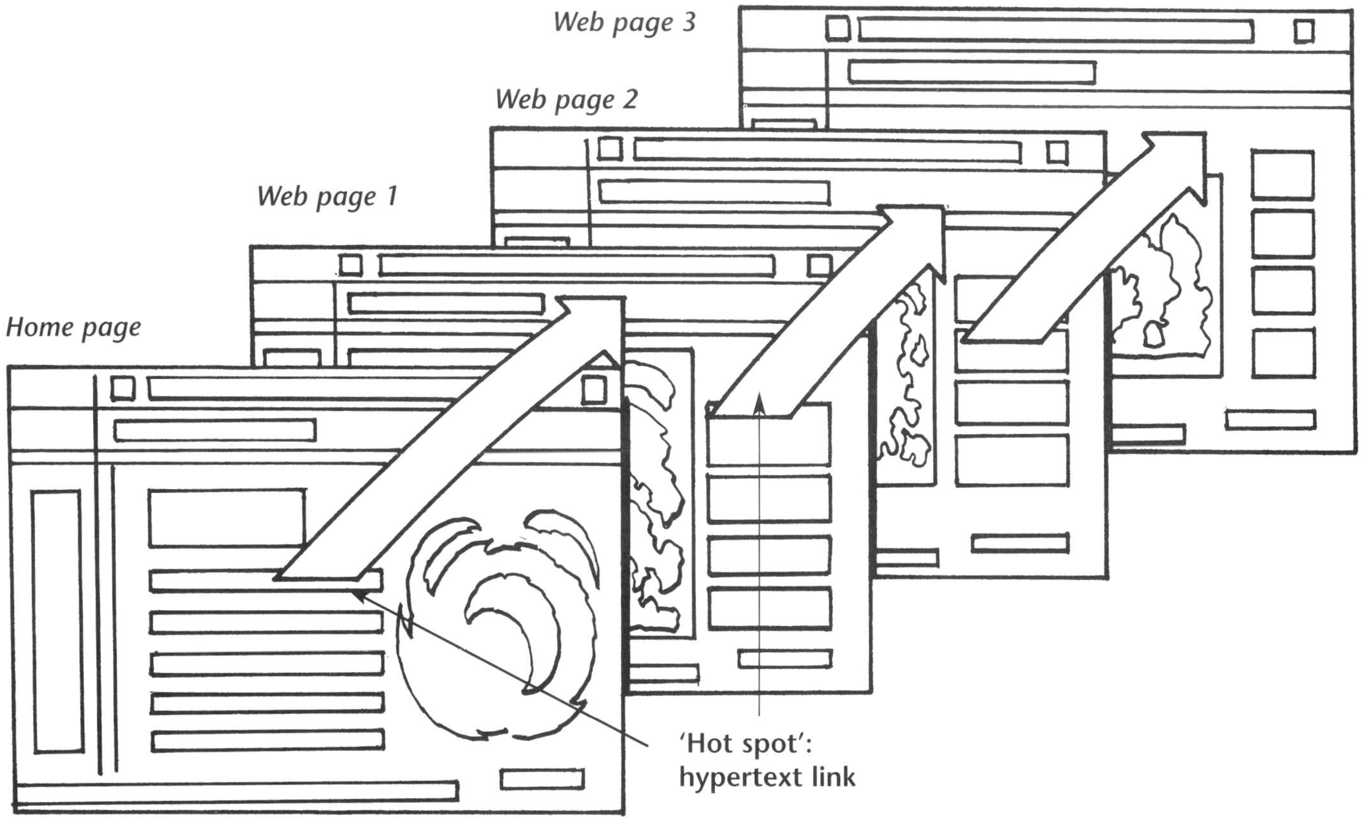

THE WEB: A NEW WORLD

These two ideas – the Internet (or system of linked computers) and hypertext – were brought together at CERN to establish the World Wide Web by 1991. It took huge corporations such as Microsoft to realise the enormous commercial and educational potential of a worldwide system of computer communications. But within the last decade the World Wide Web has penetrated everywhere. Today, it underpins all the services on which we rely.

The Internet has grown into a vast array of web sites offering everything from second-hand cars to first-class teaching resources. The motivation for this phenomenal growth – which shows little sign of slowing down – has come from millions of individuals and companies, large and small, that have realised its potential as a communicating tool.

THE FUTURE OF THE INTERNET

Many teachers and pupils now regularly use laptop computers and hand-held computing devices. Sometimes these laptops can be connected into the school network. Some forecasters suggest that the future for computer-use in education would be to equip every child with her/his own laptop to be used at home and at school. The Internet would then become the main link between home and school and between schools and their LEAs and Government Agencies.

A step towards this 'wired-up community' is the vast increase in the amount of information that can be transported over the Internet, using copper telephone wiring. This has been achieved by expanding the 'bandwidth' of signals – effectively allowing more information to pass over the Internet per second without increasing the thickness of the wires. More and more companies and institutions are using broadband technologies to increase the line capacity and send large video and audio files to suitably equipped clients.

Broadband is a development that particularly suits the cable companies. If your home has cable TV, it is worth investigating the cost of combining TV, telephone and Internet access charges in a single cable package.

Internet technology will keep improving in terms of speed and quality of delivery. What will remain the same is the urgent need for quality in resources. Children, parents and teachers will have to develop critical skills in assessing that quality and remain vigilant in protecting it.

SECTION 2:

GETTING ONLINE – THE BASICS

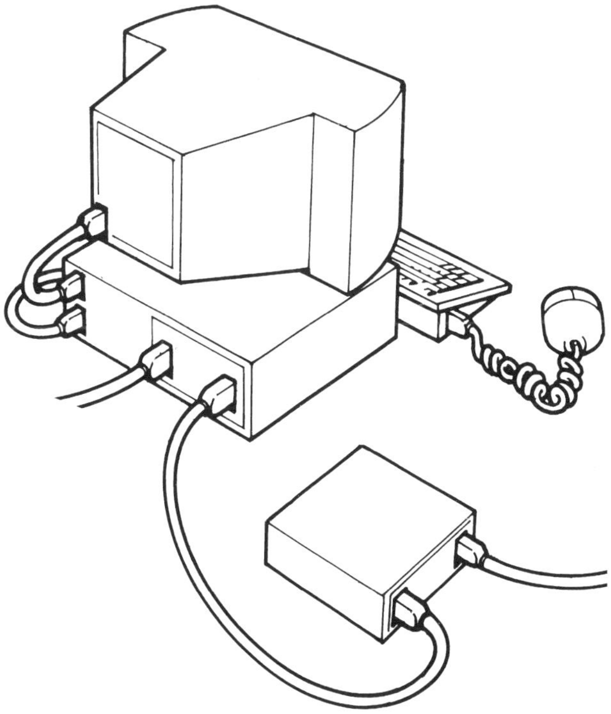

Starting up on a stand-alone PC

1 When you switch on any computer – a laptop or a stand-alone machine – the screen will settle down to look something like the one below. This is called the desktop. What appears on it will depend on the operating system. In this example, the operating system is *Windows 98*.

Desktop

These small pictures are 'active' icons – they are clickable short cuts which start applications or open files or folders.

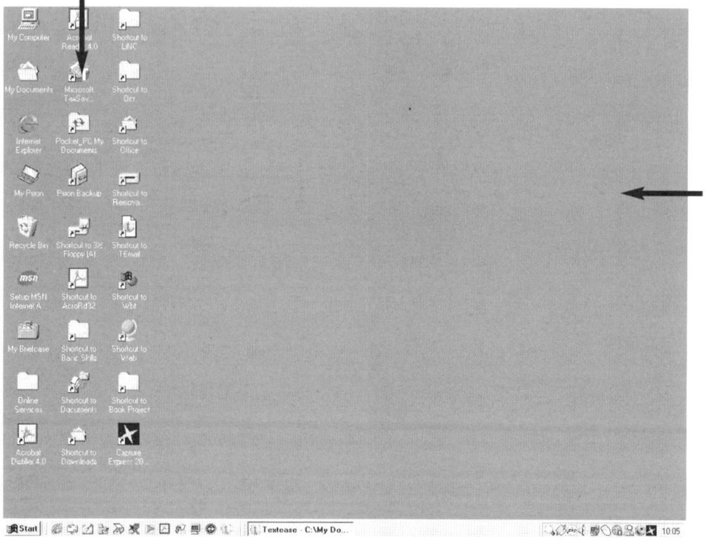

The desktop can have a different background – colour, picture or animation. These features can be accessed and changed by opening *Properties* with a right-click.

This is the *Start* button.

This is the *task bar*. It also has short cuts and shows applications currently running.

This is the *System tray*.

The start bar

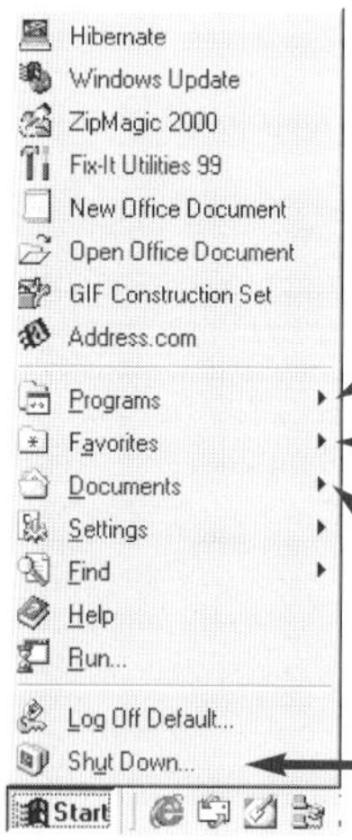

your software

visited web sites

recent documents

to end a session properly

Hints and Tips

Don't clutter your desktop with too many short cuts.

Look in your Recycle Bin and regularly clear it out.

If your task bar appears in a different place or at a different size, use a right-click on the mouse and *Properties* to restore it. Alternatively, drag it back to its original size and position.

Technical Notes

If the screen goes white, look for the clickable option to *Restore my active desktop*.

To create a short cut to an application or a folder, right-click on the icon and click this option. An active icon will appear on the desktop.

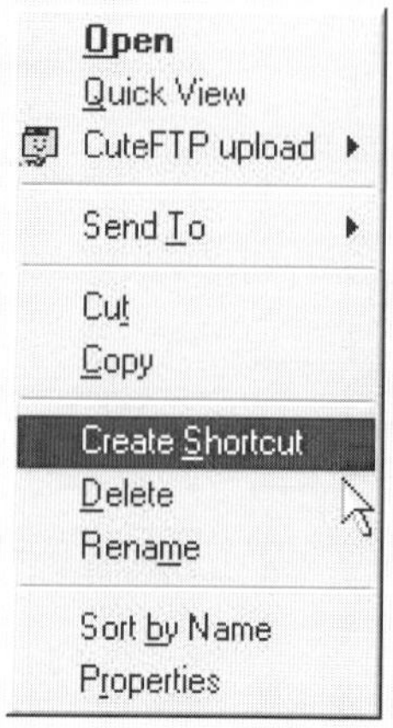

2

These are three very important short-cuts on your desktop . . .

'My Computer' shows the hard disk (C), the floppy disk drive (A), the CD ROM drive – usually (D) – and any extra drives.

'My Documents' is the area on your hard disk where your files and folders are stored.

Internet Explorer opens up your browser. This is where you click or double-click to get on to the Internet.

3

On a PC, all data is displayed in windows like the one shown here. Each window has the same features.

'maximize' button

'minimize' button

'close' button

'title' bar

'menu' bars

'status' bar

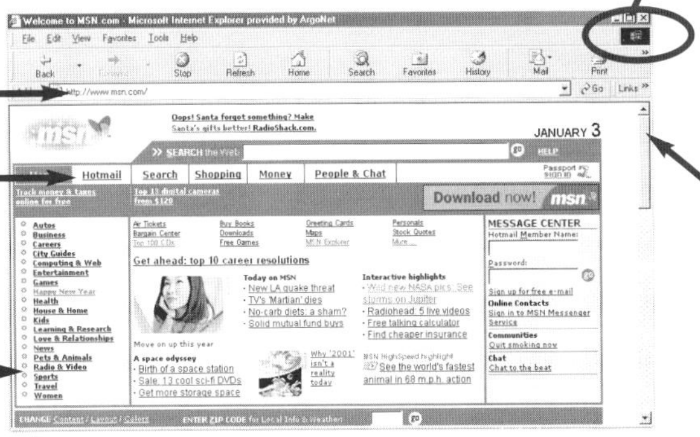

scroll bar and slider

4

Always use the *Shut Down* option to close a session or restart.

Mouse Clicks

Command	*Action*
'select'	click on an object with the left mouse button.
'double-click'	move the pointer over the chosen object and with the left mouse button click twice in quick succession.
'right-click'	click on an object with the right mouse button to view options/ 'properties' – also to rename or delete.
'drag'	move the pointer over the object to be dragged, hold down the left mouse button and move the object to its new location before releasing the button.

Hints and Tips

Your computer is set up to access the Internet along a phone line using a modem (which is probably inside the computer).
A pre-installed piece of software called a browser finds the Internet for you.

Starting up on a network PC

If your school has a network, every computer on it is linked to a central computer called a server, or 'host'. The server stores all the software and operating system and sends copies to all the networked machines. This example is based on *Internet Explorer* software and Research Machine's *Eduweb* site. (*Netscape Navigator* is another popular program used for browsing the Internet.)

HINTS AND TIPS

Type in your username and password carefully. You will have to start again if you misspell them, if you put in an extra space, or even if you use a capital letter where it should be lower case.

1 Once you have logged on to a network with your username and password, a screen like this appears.

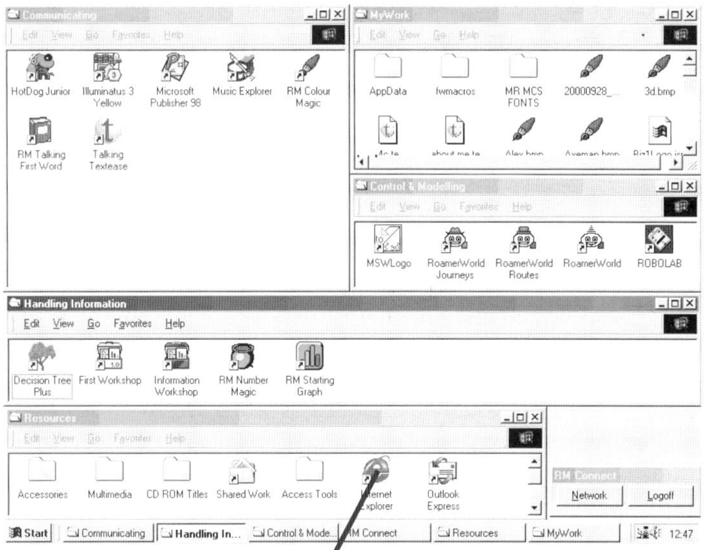

2 To get on to the Internet, look for the browser software, *Internet Explorer*.

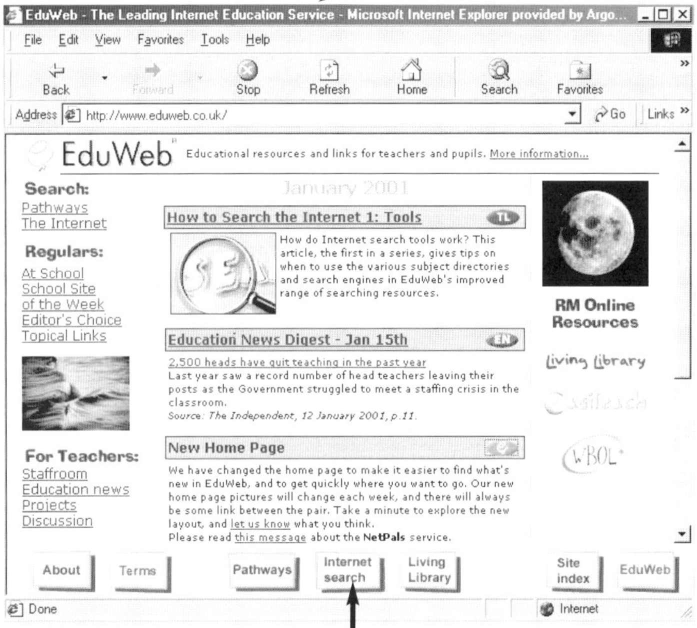

3 Click on the *Internet Explorer* icon to bring up the *Eduweb* home page. This has links to resources and other web sites.

There is also a search engine built in: Click on the *Internet search* icon.

Starting up on an Apple Macintosh

Most Primary schools use *Windows* PCs. If your school uses Apple Macintosh computers, the desktop and the opening screens for *Internet Explorer* and *Netscape Navigator* browsers will look very different from those shown opposite. However, the step-by-step techniques for exploring the World Wide Web are identical.

When you switch on an Apple Macintosh computer, the screen will settle down to look something like the one below. Double-click the mouse on the Macintosh Hard Drive icon to open the list of folders on your machine. *Internet Explorer* and *Netscape Navigator* are usually contained within the folder marked *Internet.*

Hints and Tips

The mouse used with an Apple Macintosh has only one button. Use a single click to highlight an icon and a double click to open or activate the icon or software.

This is the *Hard Drive* icon

The *Apple Icon* is located here but a different icon may appear here temporarily depending on the software you are running

The Macintosh *Desktop*

Internet Explorer Home Page

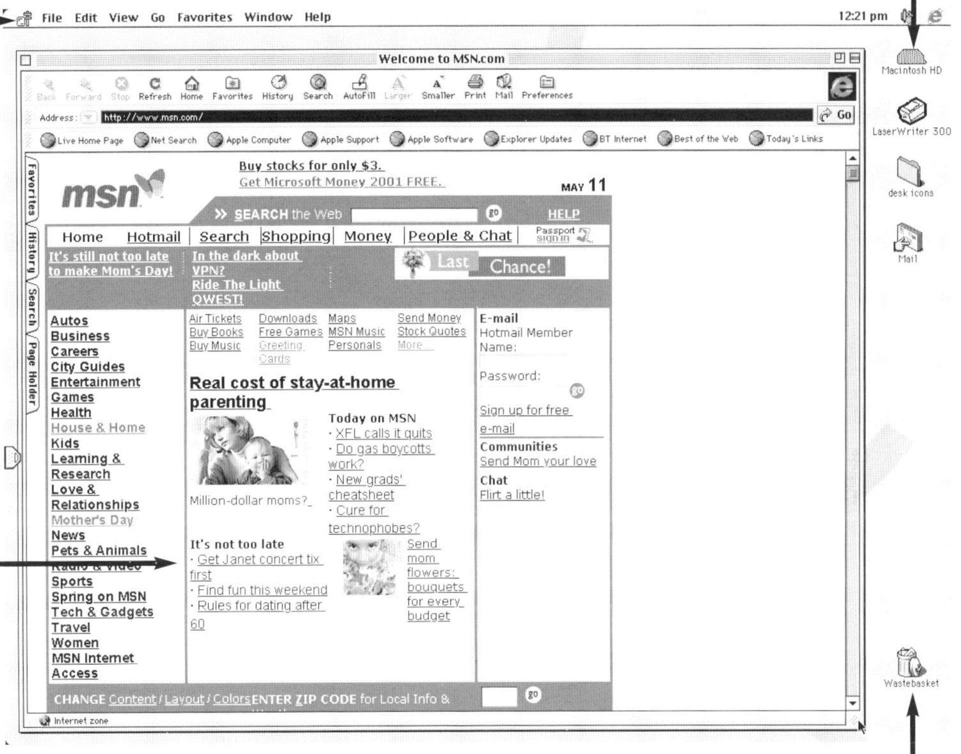

The *Wastebasket*: the Macintosh Recycle Bin

On a Macintosh you may also be able to find and open *Internet Explorer* or *Netscape Navigator* through their aliases. An 'alias' is a file that leads you quickly and simply to a specific program. When you open the alias, the original program opens. Aliases are usually found in the Apple Menu, located in the top left corner of the desktop.

1 Click on the *Apple* icon to bring up the Alias menu.

2 Drag the mouse down to the *Internet Explorer* or *Netscape Navigator* alias, then release the button. The home page will open.

Starting your browser

1 When you launch (start) your browser it will look for your service provider's home page. This is Microsoft's home page. A home page is a web site's contents page or index.

Hints and Tips

A browser is a software tool that lets you look around the World Wide Web just as you might browse in a shop or library. The most widely used browser is Microsoft's *Internet Explorer*. The one illustrated on these pages is version 5.

Back and Forward arrows to view stored web pages

Click here to start a new search

Shows a list of your favourite web sites

Button bar

Menu bar

The Address bar

Enter the URL/Address to visit a new web site

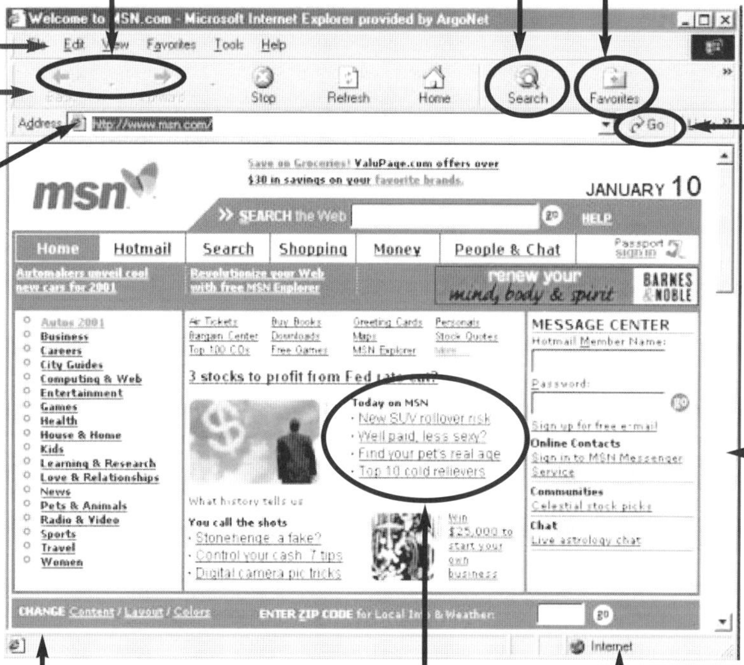

Click *Go* to open the web site in the Address bar

Scroll bar to move up and down the screen

The Status Bar gives information on current download

Hot Spots* or *Clickable Links

When the pointer changes to a 'hand', click to visit another page or web site

Zone currently accessed on the Internet

Hints and Tips

Home pages like Microsoft's are packed with information and helpful links, which may include the date, weather reports, horoscopes and so on. They include 'hotspots' (underlined words or icons) that are linked to other pages or web sites containing news, entertainment and adverts.

2 If your browser software is *Netscape Navigator*, not *Internet Explorer*, your tool bar will look different, as shown below, but the web pages you visit will look exactly the same.

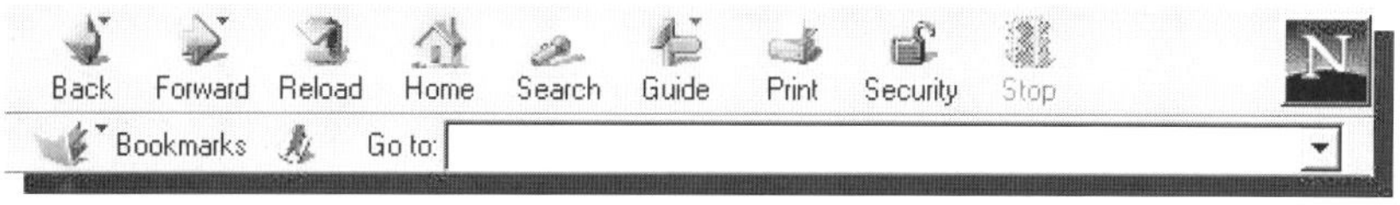

Changing your home page

1 Unless you change it, *Internet Explorer* begins each Internet session by going to the Microsoft home page shown opposite.

2 Wherever you are on the Internet you can always return to your home page by clicking on the *Home* icon.

3 If you want to change your home page, first connect to your proposed new home page. For example, you might wish to open each session at a search engine, such as *Yahoo*.

4 Click the *Tools* button and highlight *Internet Options*.

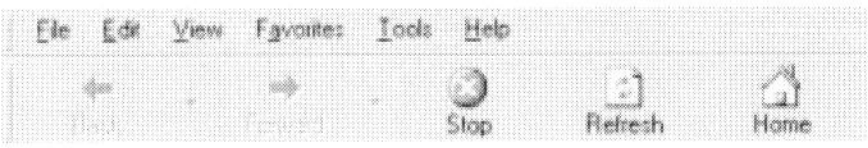

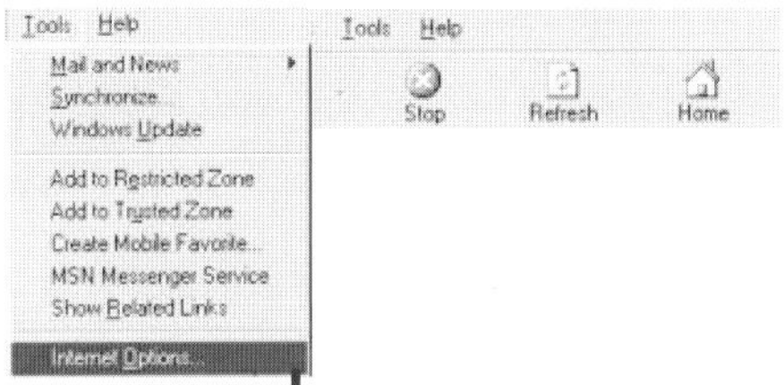

5 Click on *Use Current* to make this your new home page.

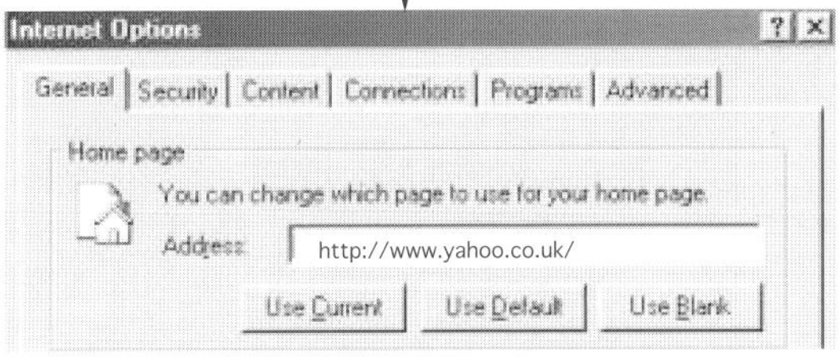

6 *Yahoo*'s home page has links to lots of other sites.

Hints and Tips

Pressing the *Function* key *F11* expands the *Explorer* window to fill your whole screen. Pressing *F11* again returns the window to its original size and position.

Technical Notes

You can find out more about *Netscape Navigator* by visiting these web sites:

Netscape Help Site
http://www.geocities.com/Athens/Forum/5122/

Netscape Browser Archive
http://sillydog.webhanger.com/archive

On page 90, in Recommended Web sites, we have listed several other good search engines you can use at school.

Accessing a web page

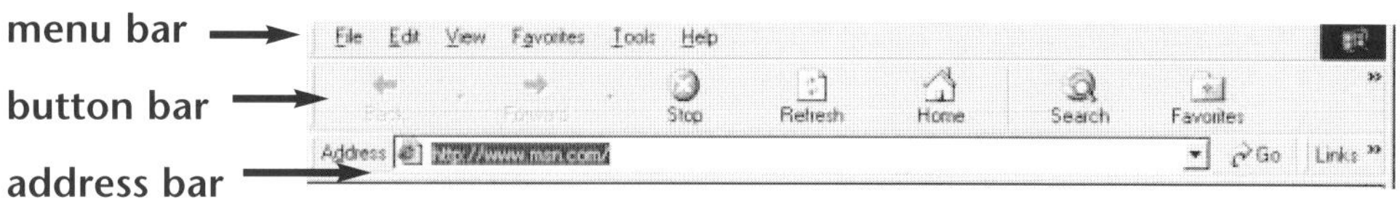

Web addresses (URLs)

Every web site has its own address called a URL (universal resource locator). Once your browser has taken you to your home page, you will see a set of 'bars' at the top of your *Internet Explorer* window like the ones shown above.

The address bar is where you type the URL of a web site you want to visit. Suppose you want to go to the home page of SITE Training Services. The full address has three parts:

http://www.sitetraining.com/index.htm

http://	is the 'protocol name' showing this is a web page
www.sitetraining.com	is the 'host name': the name of the web site where the pages you want to visit are stored
/index.htm	is the file path showing where the page is stored.

You do not have to type the full address every time you want to travel on the Internet. When you use your mouse to click in the address bar, anything already there will be highlighted in blue and all you have to do is type the host name, **www.sitetraining.com** – *Internet Explorer* will automatically add the rest of the URL.

All you need to do now is click on the *Go* button or press the ENTER key on your keyboard. Don't be surprised if you have to wait a while. Access to the World Wide Web is getting faster all the time but the telephone lines are often busy.

Hints and Tips

Do not forget that you have to be online to put in a URL for a web page.

Type the URL carefully (check upper and lower cases and spaces) exactly as it should be written.

Do not be put off if the browser appears to be trying to finish the address for you. It is an 'intuitive' piece of software and stores commonly used web site addresses.

When working with children, it is a good idea to have an alternative site to visit, in case the one you are aiming for is busy and takes too long to load.

Technical Notes

The first page on any web site is saved either with the filename 'homepage' or 'index'.

What the suffix letters mean:

.ac	academic/ educational
.co	company
.com	commercial
.gov	government
.org	organisation
.net	internet company

'Favorites': saving a page link

Internet Explorer has a way of saving the addresses of your favourite web sites, so that you do not have to type the URL each time. For example, you might want to revisit a site that has regular software upgrades or useful classroom resources. This saving process is called 'bookmarking' because it 'keeps your place' on the Internet.

1 First connect to the web site that you want to bookmark. In this example, it is **www.softease.com**

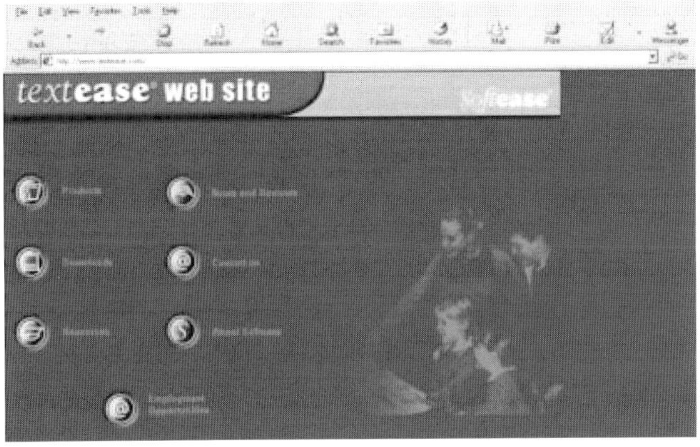

2 When the web site home page opens, click the Favorites button . . .

and an extra window will open on the left of your screen.

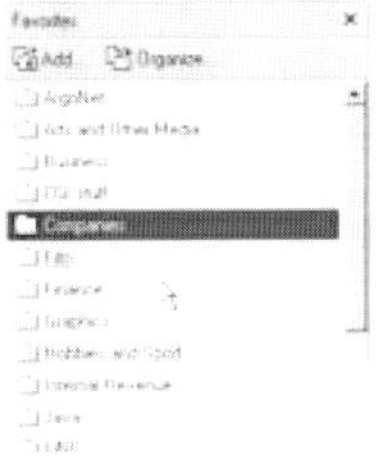

It will probably have different folders showing but the bar at the top will still be the same.

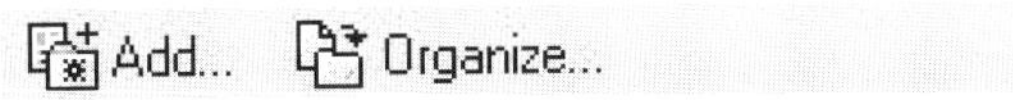

3 Clicking **Add...** will bring up this new window.

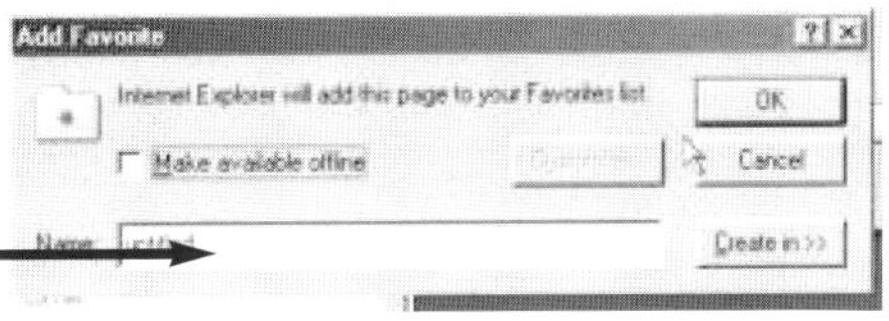

Name field →

4 Click on the *Name* field, then type in a suitable name for the link, such as the company name. Use the *Create in* button to open up the lower half of this window, where you can find a suitable folder in which to save this link, or create a new folder for this type of link.

Hints and Tips

Saving favourite web sites really makes sense if everyone using the machine joins in.

In a school there needs to be some discussion about what kinds of link to save and how to organise the links so that everyone can access them easily.

The short-cut way to add a favourite web site is to hold down CONTROL and press the 'D' key.

Technical Notes

Netscape has its own way of saving links to specific web pages, using *Bookmarks*. To add a page in *Netscape Navigator*, open the menu called *Bookmarks* and click on *Add Bookmark*.

Some web pages may be worth saving to your hard disk because they contain information you will want to use over and over again. Saving web pages is called downloading, and is explained in the following sections.

Organising bookmarked sites

'Favorites' can be reorganised into appropriate and useful folders, for example by subject or by topic.

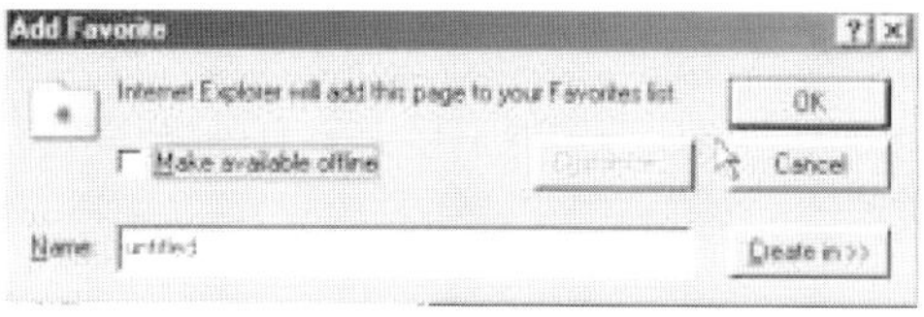

1 The *Add Favorite* dialogue box has a *Create in>>* button which leads to an extension where you can open up an existing folder or create a new one to suit your needs.

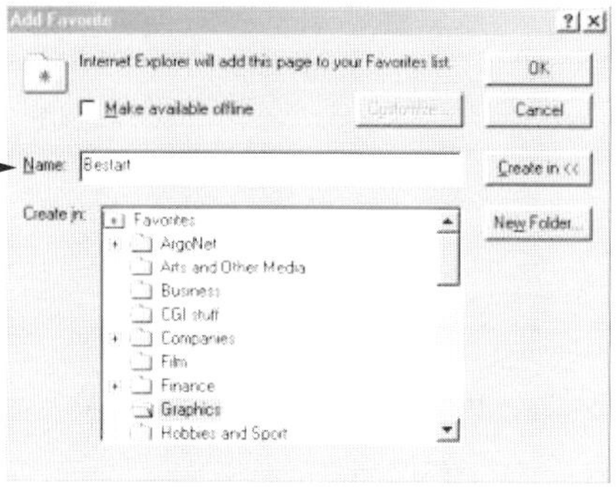

2 Click here to select a sub folder in which to save your 'favorite' link and give it a name.

Confirm your selection by clicking *OK*.

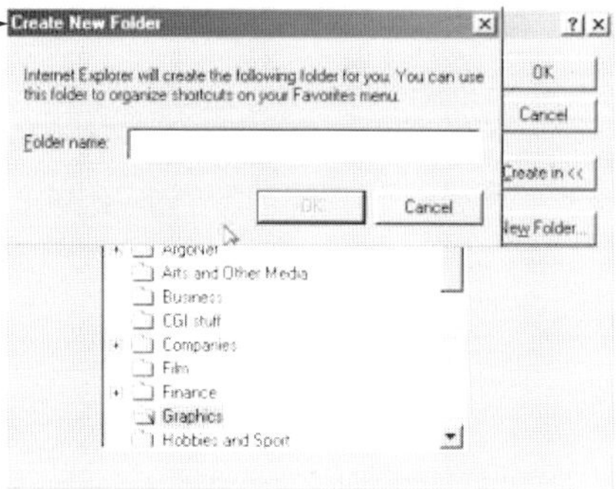

3 OR click here to make a new folder. A new dialogue box appears.

4 Type in the name of your new folder here. The *OK* button will become active. Click *OK* to add your new folder to the list of other sub folders.

5 Another way to view a list of *Favorites* is via the *Start* button. Once your *Favorites* are showing, double-click on an address to go there (provided you are online).

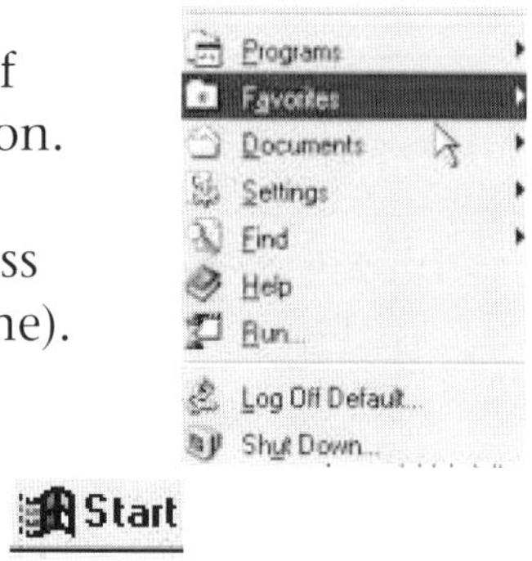

Hints and Tips

If your school has an Intranet and/or a web site, these links can be updated and displayed regularly for everyone.

If you see an address on an e-mail or a word-processed page, you can highlight it by dragging the mouse with the left button held down, then use CONTROL and the 'C' key to copy it to the clipboard.

Paste this URL directly into the address bar by clicking and pressing CONTROL and the 'V' key. Then press ENTER and your browser will take you to the web address.

Technical Notes

Windows in which you type instructions (like those shown on this page) are called dialogue boxes.

By clicking on a button in a dialogue box, you can create an 'extension' where further instructions can be typed.

Where a folder contains other sub folders, you will see a '+' sign. Click on this sign to view the list of sub folders.

Starting a search

If you are unsure of an exact web site address, you will need to use a search engine such as *Google*, *Yahoo* or *Ask Jeeves* (see page 90) to find your way through the vast bank of web sites on the Internet.

For an introduction to searching the Internet, visit the National Grid for Learning (NGfL) web site – **www.ngfl.gov.uk**. This has a directory, a search engine and links to many educational routes through the Internet.

1 Key in the address of the National Grid for Learning, **www.ngfl.gov.uk**.

2 This is the *nglf* home page. Make yourself familiar with the various parts of the page.

These are 'tabs' leading to other pages.

This is where you can type in a keyword to activate the search engine on the site.

These are categories of special interest to teachers.

Directory of further index links

Information about the content of a web site is kept in the form of relevant keywords. These are decided by the web designer when she or he builds the web site. For example, some of the keywords describing a web site about pond life may be 'pond', 'frog', 'dragonfly' and 'life cycle'. The designer encodes these keywords in an index page and the words are picked up by passing spiders.

When you are searching for particular information on the Internet, you have to reverse the process and try to guess which keywords would describe a web site containing the information you need. You do not need to know the URL or address of the site, just have some idea of its contents.

Hints and Tips

A search engine really is just a huge list or index, compiled by special programs called 'spiders'. Spiders crawl around the Internet looking for information about the location, title and content of web pages.

As well as 'spiders', most search engines have another kind of list called a directory. This is a series of useful categories into which web sites are divided. Directories often make a good starting point in a search for information.

A search example: the Tudors

1 To find information and resources on the Tudors, begin on the NGfL home page by typing in a general keyword search such as 'history' or by clicking on *Learning Resource Index* then *History* to reach the page shown.

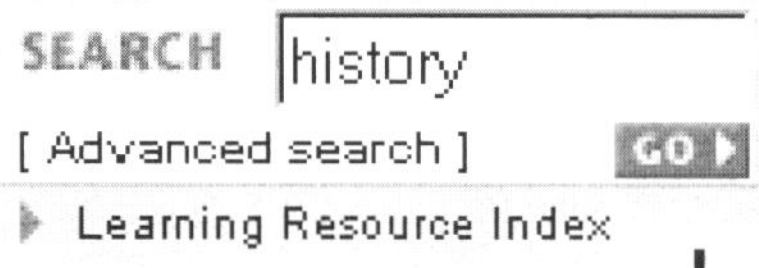

2 The search engine brings up a range of web sites.

3 Click on the hyperlink that seems the most useful or relevant. **www.icteachers.co.uk** is a good site with plenty of subject resources and links.

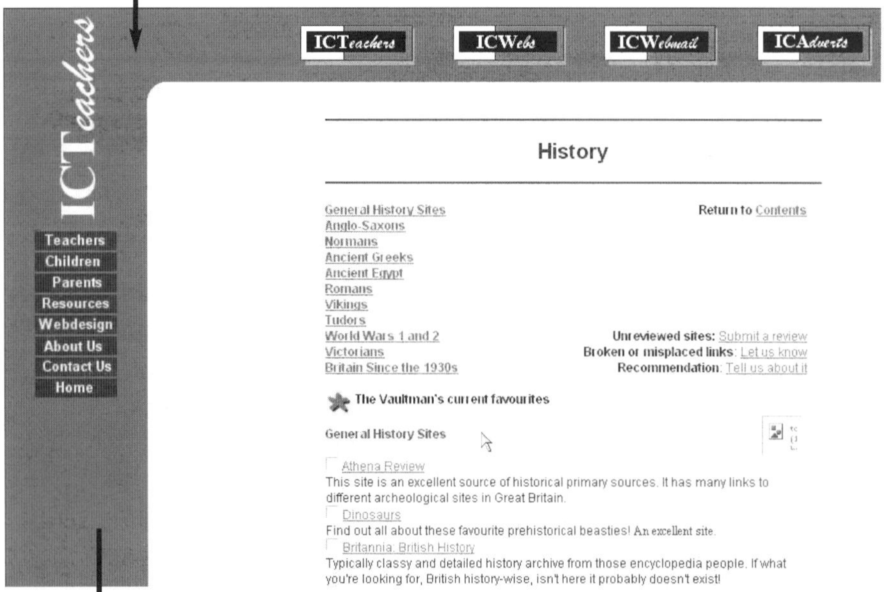

4 Click on the *Tudors* link to bring up an index of useful Tudor sites (see next page).

Hints and Tips

Think carefully about keywords and key phrases.

Correct spelling is crucial.

Every search engine has its own *Advanced Search* options to help in refining your enquiry.

There is usually a GO button next to or near the search window. Once you have typed in your keyword, click on this GO button or press ENTER from the keyboard.

Web sites on particular themes are often linked – sometimes in a 'web ring'. So, if one site does not have what you want, look for a clickable list of other related sites.

Most windows display a status bar at the bottom of the screen. You can use this to check the speed of the download as the bar fills up from left to right.

Sometimes the bar will appear to have stopped moving. BE PATIENT – it may continue. If it has stalled, repeat the process.

5 Click again on one of the *Tudors* links.

Hints and Tips

When doing a search, copy your keyword or phrase on to the clipboard (by pressing CONTROL and the 'C' key). You can paste it back into the search box by pressing CONTROL and the 'V' key; then highlight it to make small changes. Or you can paste it into a different search engine.

6 Click again to take you further into the site.

7 On arrival here, you or the children can follow further internal links which will help you to find the information you are looking for. Clicking on the images at thc top of this screen will take you to pages showing details of each monarch.

Keyword searches and how to refine them

In the previous example, where the keyword 'History' was used, we took advantage of a site that was organised by subjects and had been designed to lead to an index list of UK educational sites. However, sometimes we may want to use a more refined keyword search using, for example, the phrase "Tudor food" in order to find the answer to 'What was the Tudors' favourite food?'

This example is on **www.yahoo.co.uk**

1

2

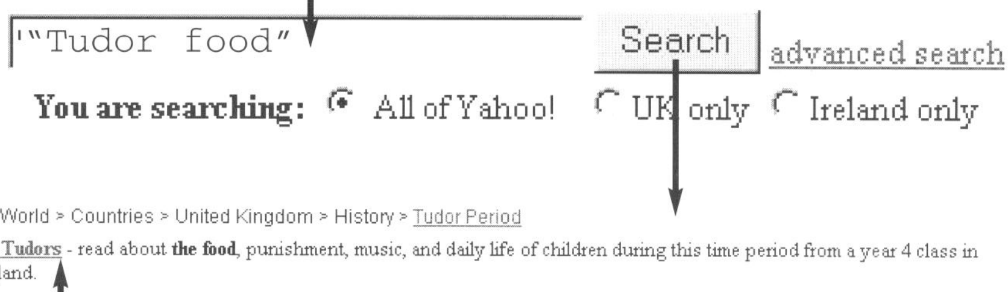

3 Click this link and you'll see what children at this school have already found out about the Tudors.

Our books are for future year four children when they are studying the Tudors and we hope they enjoy reading them and that they will help them. We decided to put the books on the web for other children in other schools. If the information is not accurate please write to us and blame our teachers.

Hints and Tips

If you want to ensure that a word must appear in the results, use the '+' (plus) sign directly in front of the important word.

For example, if you enter **Tudor food** the search would return all sites or pages that contain *either* or *both* these words.

If you enter **Tudor+food** all sites or pages will contain both words. But there is no guarantee that the words will be next to each other.

To search for Tudor history specifically, you must enclose the words in speech marks, creating the phrase **"Tudor food"**

To ensure that your search does not include a certain word, place the minus (–) sign directly in front of the word you do not want the search to include.

When the list of search results appears, check the list of top hits, to eliminate the poor hits or refine your keyword or phrase. Do not assume the best hits always appear at the top of the list.

Downloading text and pictures

To use information from a web site and store it for future use, first you have to download the material on to your computer. Then you can save it in any document or file.

1 Using the theme of the Tudors as an example, go to the home page of the Tudor History web site at **http://tudorhistory.org/**

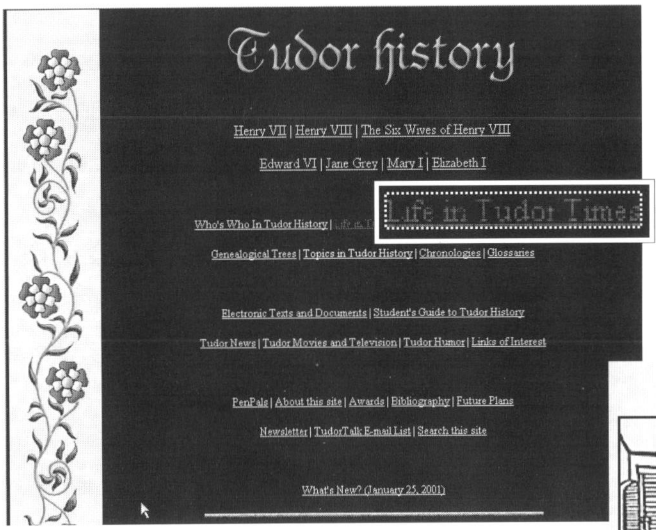

The pages and resources on this site are © Lara E. Eakins

2 Follow the links until you come to the category you are seeking: in this case, Tudor Food.

FOOD IN TUDOR ENGLAND

3 Clicking on hotspots opens up web pages with pictures and text.

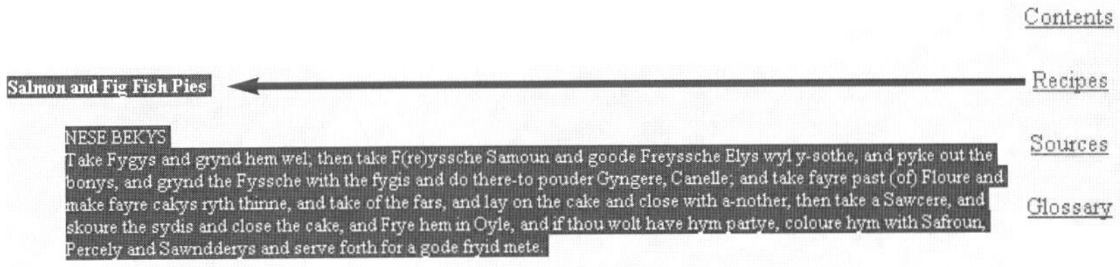

4 Highlight the section of text you want to download by clicking at the start of the first sentence and holding down the right mouse button while moving to the end of the text.

5 A further right-click shows this menu. Click on the highlighted *Copy* option.

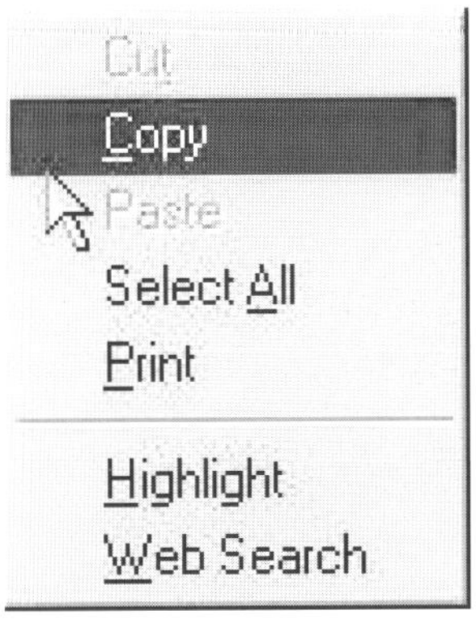

6 The recipe text has been copied to the clipboard. From here it can be pasted into any application. Use the same steps to download pictures.

Hints and Tips

The clipboard is a temporary storage area on your computer to where text and pictures can be downloaded. The short-cut is to highlight the text or picture and press CONTROL and the 'C' key.

If you have a word processor or desktop publisher application running while you are on the Internet – perhaps minimised on the task bar – simply open up the writing area and use the short-cut of pressing CONTROL and the 'V' key to paste in the copied text or image.

On page 41 there is an example of a web site link to the *Mary Rose Trust* and downloads on Tudor history, geography, art and science and technology.

Technical Note

Where possible, check that you are free to use material downloaded from a web site. Look for details of copyright on the web site.

Providing you are using material for educational and not commercial purposes, it is usually safe for you to use text and pictures from a web site in your work.

Printing

You can print out any page directly from a web site, with text, pictures or both. Before you try and print any text (or images), make sure your printer is switched on and has paper in it. Some printers will take a minute or two to warm up: there may be an orange 'stand-by' light that will change to a green 'on' light when the printer is ready.

Hints and Tips

Check your printer options. You may be able to use different print qualities – from 'rough' or 'draft' to 'normal' – and print at various reductions and enlargements. By using draft quality and printing at reduced size, you will save on printer toner. Pictures use up far more toner than text.

1 Clicking the *Print* option means that a dialogue box will appear, asking you how many copies of all the pages you require.

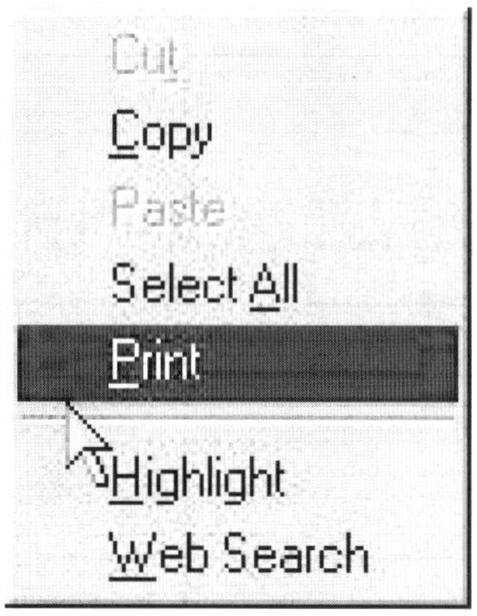

2 Decide how much of the text on a web page you need to print. The 'Print range' options are usually:
'All': to print the whole web document, which can run into many pages.
'Pages from': where you have to insert page numbers and
'Selection': to print whatever is highlighted. (See page 40.)

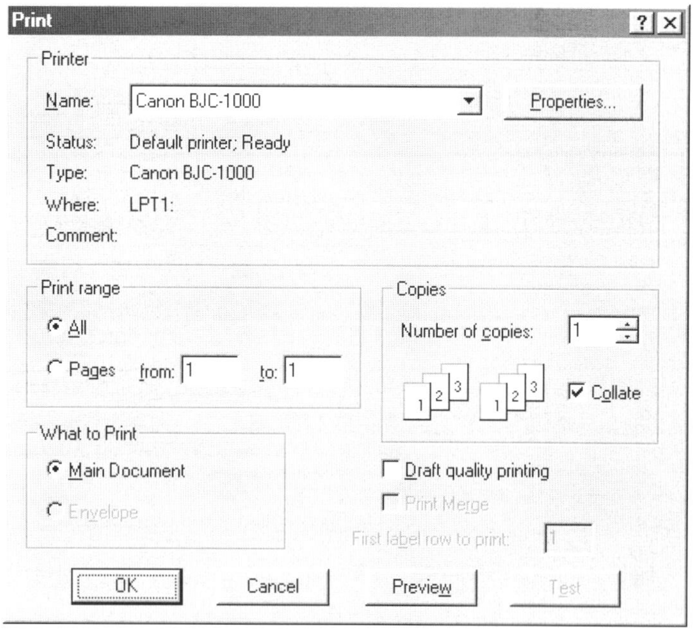

3 If you want to print out just the highlighted section of text, copy it to your word processor document and do it from there.

Saving and copying a picture

To store downloaded material, you need to save it on your hard disk.

1 Click the right mouse button over the picture you want to save and bring up this menu:

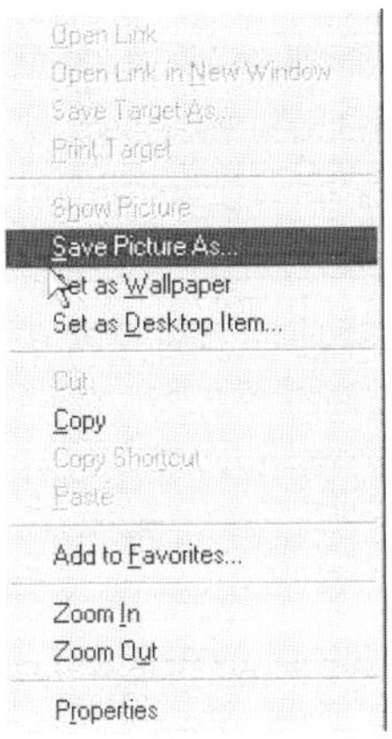

2 Highlight the *Save Picture As . . .* option and click.

3 You will then see a *Save as . . .* dialogue box. Follow the instructions to save in a format that suits your needs. (see Hints and Tips opposite.) You can save text in a similar way.

Hints and Tips

Images can be saved in different formats such as JPEG, TIFF and GIF.

JPEG is the standard compressed format for higher resolution images; it takes up less space when stored. TIFF is a widely used Apple format. GIF is the standard lower resolution image format used in web pages.

When saving items, be sure to name their files so you can retrieve them easily.

Copying a picture

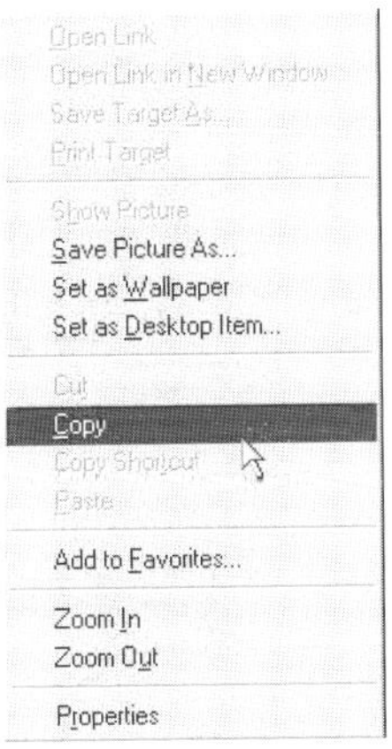

1 To copy a downloaded picture, right-click on it to bring up the same menu. This time, highlight the *Copy* option and click.

2 The picture has now been copied to the clipboard. From here, it can be pasted into any application on your hard disk.

Using Internet text in a word-processing program

You can create classroom resources by cutting and pasting or copying useful text from web sites. In this example a poster has been prepared for a science lesson using *Word 2000* with a space left for material downloaded from the Internet.

Hints and Tips

Use a right-button click over a web page text or graphic to bring up the options for copying, selecting and printing.

Minimise a word-processed file to the Task Bar while you are copying from the Internet, ready to be opened up when you copy or insert text or graphics.

1 Write your instructions to the children in the *Word* document.

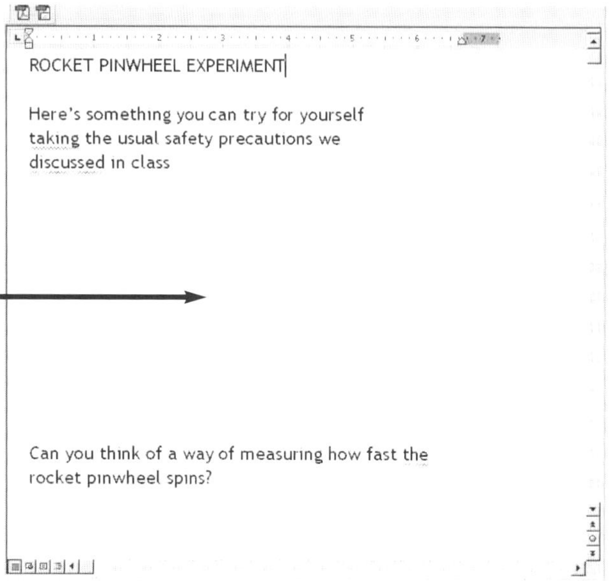

The instructions are to be copied from a web site and pasted here.

2 Find the text you want to download. We found this experiment by following the science-spacecraft links from **http://sunsite.berkeley.edu/KidsClick!**

3 Drag the mouse across the text you want to highlight.

4 A right-button click now shows the option to *Copy*.

5 Open the *Word* file and click in the appropriate space.

6 Use CONTROL–V to insert text or edit and paste from the menu bar.

Using Internet images in a desktop publishing program

In this example, a document has been prepared for a history lesson using *Word 2000* with a space left for a map downloaded from the Internet. Material was used from the web site of the *Mary Rose Trust*: **http://www.maryrose.org/**

1 Write your introductory text in the *Word* document.

The image to be copied from a web site and pasted here.

2 Following *The Learning City* link through the History pages of the web site, this map can be found.

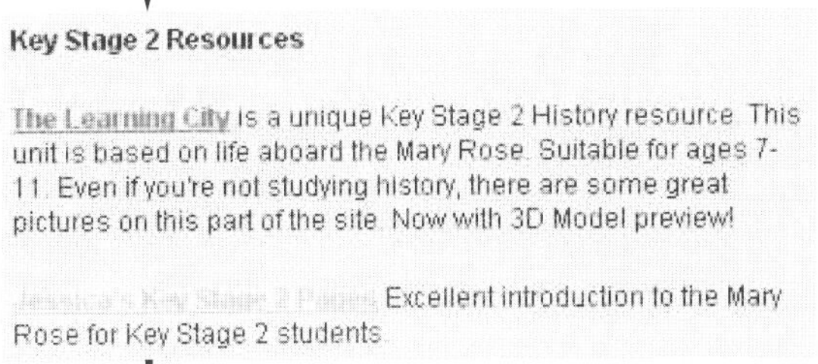

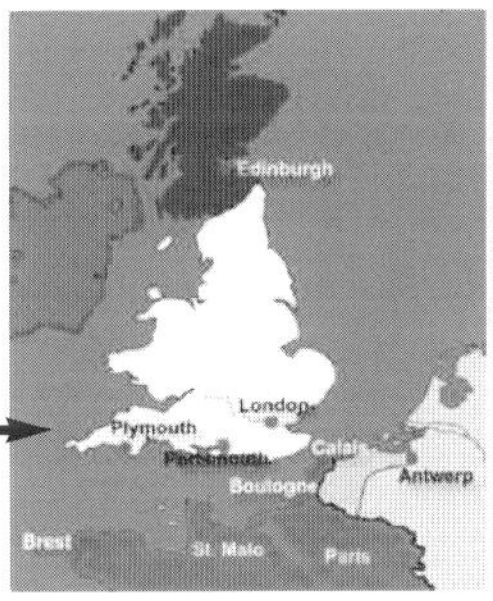

3 Right-click the mouse over the image on the web site page and highlight the *Copy* option. The image can then be pasted into the reopened *Word* document.

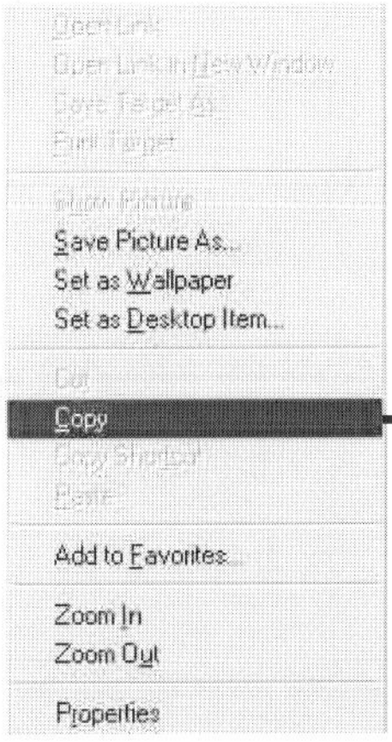

Joining Newsgroups

The proper name for a newsgroup is a 'Usenet discussion group'. It is just a collection of like-minded enthusiasts. There are thousands of newsgroups using the Usenet system, having ongoing discussions about subjects from dinosaurs to oceanography. You can also use newsgroups to exchange information about useful web sites or new search engines you have found.

1 Start *Outlook Express* and a window like the one below will open.

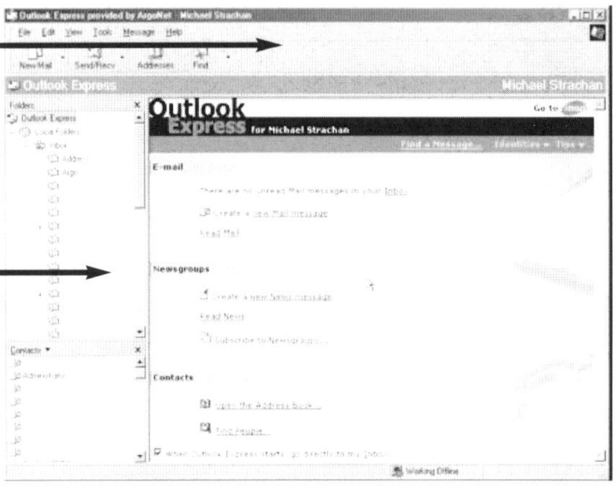

2 Click here to start the process of becoming a subscriber to newsgroups.

3 Insert a keyword here that best describes the kind of newsgroup you want to find.

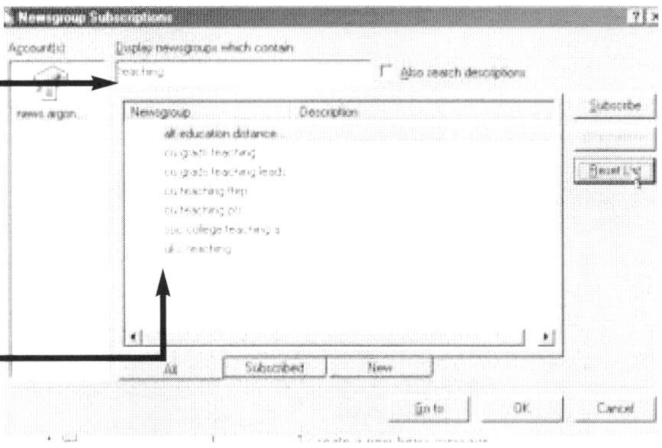

4 A list of groups will appear here and you can click to select one.

5 Narrow your search keyword before you press the *Subscribe* button or you will have to wait while thousands of groups download. In this example, the keyword 'teachers' produced over 30,000 newsgroups to choose from.

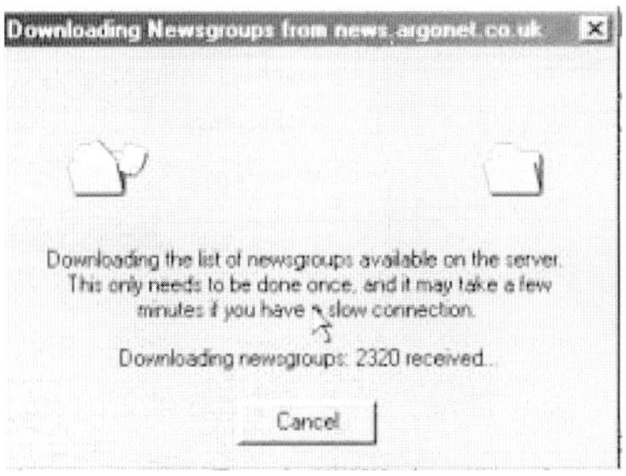

Hints and Tips

The types of newsgroups you can have access to, or subscribe to, depends on your Internet Service Provider.

Technical Notes

To read articles you need a piece of software called a *Newsreader*. It is built into *Outlook Express* in recent versions of *Windows*.

Downloading the list of newsgroups that your IAP provides can take many minutes but only needs to be done once.

Hints and Tips

Hundreds of newsgroups are created each day. It is impossible to monitor all of them. Many are not suitable for children or for use in school. Use only those newsgroups recommended by education authorities or trusted teachers or adults.

Use a filtered service whenever possible, but make checks regularly.

SECTION 3:
QUESTIONS AND ANSWERS

Q What Can I Do When The Equipment Fails?

A Computers sometimes 'freeze' or 'crash'. The more up-to-date your operating system, the less likely this is to happen. Holding down the CONTROL and ALT keys and pressing the DELETE key will usually identify the fault and the system may provide advice on what to do next.

If nothing appears to work, consult your manual about using the re-set button. This is a small button, usually concealed in a recess that closes down and restarts your computer. When the computer starts up, you will almost certainly see a blue warning screen with a message about checking your hard disk for error. Don't panic – the message usually clears without any further problem.

If you are using a network and everything seizes up, make the ICT co-ordinator or network manager aware but don't restart or switch off the computer. Leave it so the manager can read any warning message that has appeared on screen.

Hints and Tips

To identify any possible fault, start at the most basic source of trouble such as power supply, plugs and fuses, loose connections.

Ensure all separate pieces of equipment – monitor, printer, scanner (sometimes called peripherals) – are connected and switched on before starting up.

Q What Can I Do About Software Problems And Viruses?

A Many unexpected software problems that produce strange 'error messages' on screen can be sorted out by closing down your machine and restarting it. If possible, log off the network or shut down your machine in the proper way.

Viruses can find their way into your hard drive and corrupt your software or operating software. One precaution against viruses is to avoid, or restrict the use of, floppy disks. Many schools now do this. Ensure your system is equipped with an up-to-date virus checker for examining disks and files. You can download the latest versions of anti-virus software from the Internet.

Hints and Tips

Go online regularly to update your virus-checking software.

Q How Can I Avoid Losing An Internet Connection?

A Browsers such as *Internet Explorer* and *Netscape Navigator* are complex pieces of software and prone to unexpected glitches. Keep track of where you are, for example by bookmarking sites or jotting down URLs, so that you can get back to a site easily after a crash. Sometimes a lost connection can be sorted out by pressing the REFRESH button at the top of the screen page.

Q How Can I Avoid Traffic Jams On The Internet?

A Start by considering why you are experiencing a traffic jam. It could just be that there are too many people trying to use your provider's computers and all the lines are engaged. Until the widespread availability of 'broadband' services, this problem will persist. Video and sound files are popular downloads and they are often made up of huge amounts of data. That's how Internet 'traffic jams' can happen.

There seem to be certain times of day when it's difficult to get online, and you just have to try a little later. For example, the time when people in the UK are checking their e-mail and exploring the Internet in the early evening, when phone fees are low, corresponds with people in the United States waking up and doing the same.

Don't forget that small Internet Service Providers may simply not have enough telephone lines to service all their customers at one time. Bigger providers or Internet access providers have more lines and bigger servers.

Hints and Tips

Where possible, stagger Internet access to avoid large groups trying to access the same site at the same time.

If the problem continues and access is denied, or is very slow, have some alternative classroom activities available.

If access is denied, it is worth trying the REFRESH button.

Q Why Am I Experiencing Address Problems?

A A common reason for not getting to your Internet destination is typing in the wrong URL. One small mistake – such as mixing up upper-case and lower-case letters, or using the wrong character – could take you to a dead-end.

If you are trying to reach the web site of a large, well-known company or institution, it's likely that, even if the address of the site changes, you'll be provided with a link to the new one. On the other hand, many smaller sites just disappear – perhaps the authors have just lost interest and moved on to other things.

Hints and Tips

Regularly inspect the mouse by removing the rubber ball and cleaning the contacts carefully.

To make profitable use of helplines, you need to have sufficient basic skills and understanding of technology to follow the directions you will be given.

Don't hesitate to ask the helpline operative to explain things in simple terms.

Q What Type Of Hardware Problems Can I Fix And How?

A The good news is that you don't have to be a computer expert to keep things going. Here are a few tips.

- If you switch on your computer at home or in the classroom and nothing happens, first check whether the plugs to the main power supply are secure and switched on.
- If you come back to a computer that has been in use and the screen is blank, it may just be that it is in power-saving mode. Jiggle the mouse and the screen may reappear.

• If a printer stops working, check that the ink cartridges or toner cartridge are not empty and that there is sufficient dry, clean, uncreased paper in the feeder.

If the problem persists, speak to someone more experienced.

Q Where Can I Find Help When I Need It?

A If you are a classroom teacher, then your first port of call is your ICT network manager, co-ordinator or more experienced colleague. If your LEA has an advisory service, you can approach them for help.

Some LEAs use private agencies and companies for support and training. Your advisory teacher should be able to point you in the right direction.

Alternatively, some schools use an independent advisor, who will regularly visit the school and offer practical help with hardware and software.

Network managers and ICT co-ordinators should have an ISP hotline or be able to call on the installation company to sort out some problems.

Q Where Can I Find Help When I Am At Home?

A If you have signed up with an Internet Access Provider or Internet Service Provider that has a free support hotline, try calling the number. Usually, someone at the other end will take you through each step of the installation process and supply any missing information. Unfortunately, if you are using only one telephone line for your Internet and home uses, this can prove difficult. Another problem can be that lines are often engaged.

Q Can Pupils Break The Security Of The Internet?

A It is possible, with the right level of skill, to hack into any part of the Internet, or a network. However, under the watchful eyes of teachers at school and parents at home, children are not likely to break Internet security systems. What pupils *can* easily do, however, is:

- change the start-up appearance of the desktop
- download dangerous files
- overwork/confuse the browser software

Usually if aspects of the desktop have been changed (such as the position of the task bar or *Start* button) the original configuration can be restored without too much trouble.

But downloading software can be dangerous. It is possible to add an application to your computer that conflicts with something already on your system. Stick to guaranteed sites and companies when hunting down new software, or install only from CD-ROMs, and you should be safe. Your ICT co-ordinator may also have her/his own policy on downloading software which is, don't do it!

If you have an Internet policy in place within the school and if parents use a filtered system and occasionally monitor what children are using and how often, then you are taking reasonable precautions.

In Section 5 of the book, Recommended Web sites, we have provided some links to LEAs and agencies who provide specimen policies that schools can use and develop for their own needs.

Q What Is Involved In Security, Passwords and Filtering Information?

A It is advisable, particularly in school, to link up to an Internet Access Provider who has already looked at ways of preventing children accessing unsuitable sites and influences.

Generally speaking, this involves blocking or filtering certain keywords. It guarantees some peace of mind but it is not infallible. Parents and teachers need to be on guard and monitor the parts of the Internet that children visit.

Encouraging children to be critical in judging the worth of material on the Internet is probably the best guarantee in the long run that they will not be harmed by what they see and read.

An Internet Policy Document discussed and agreed with all parties is essential.

Hints and Tips

Network managers need to carefully monitor sites visited.

Do not give out any personal, private or financial information unless you are guaranteed security by the organisation you have contacted.

Whatever system is used to create passwords, it should be consistent.

Q How Can I Make The Most Of Limited Resources?

A In the majority of schools, teachers have to timetable computer use with great care. If there is just one computer in a classroom, collaborative work with small groups of children working on directed tasks is the best option.

Even where a network of computers exists together in one classroom, this resource still has to be carefully timetabled to provide equal access to the largest number of pupils. These issues need to be discussed together by all teaching staff.

When on a limited budget, consider the issues of hardware and software. It is not necessary to upgrade to a later version of a program each time one comes out. Make sure you buy to suit your own needs.

Free software (often called 'freeware') is widely available, as is 'shareware'. Often, these are provided on a trial basis. The idea is that you will experiment with part of the software of the full package, and then buy the whole version when you realise you like it. Look for this type of free trial software on the Internet before buying a new program.

Another way to save time and money is to use software that schools recommend. You might find that your children's school can get you a better deal on a licensed package.

Hints and Tips

Always have a focused task so children don't waste time searching aimlessly.

Be aware that the 'freeware' or 'shareware' sites may be subsidised by advertising which can be intrusive in a school situation.

SECTION 4: Photocopiable Projects

Teachers' notes

The following photocopiable activities are designed to help children practise ICT skills in topic work across the Curriculum. The projects encourage children to critically evaluate web sites and information. They also link with literacy work in helping children to improve their research skills, providing frameworks by which the children can plan what they want to find out and record the information they find. The activity sheets are assessment tools and provide records of good web sites to use again.

Many of the activities start offline and involve the use of other resources, such as books or CD-ROMs. The icon shown here indicates the

parts of the activity sheet that need to be completed online. Most of the projects can be completed by children working in groups. They are designed to be used flexibly; for example, some members of a group could work on one part using books while other members focus on a different part and use the computer. It is not expected that the activities will be completed in one lesson, and at the end of each sheet there is a suggestion for a **Next step**, or a way of extending the project. Many of the suggestions involve planning for a group project, which may be completed over several lessons.

The following notes provide suggestions for ways of making the most of the activities and introducing, adapting or extending them.

What's on the Internet? (page 53)
Before the children begin the activity, discuss with them what is meant by the term 'information'. You could start by asking the children about their own experiences of using the Internet and what they use it for. This data could be recorded as a class graph. Then ask them if they can think of anything that other members of their family might use the Internet for. For the Next step, provide web site addresses for weather forecast (see page 89), estate agent (see page 56) and Roman history sites (see page 89).The children could discuss their findings with the whole class.

Whom is the Internet for? (page 54)
The aim of this activity is to help the children to appreciate different audiences. This is good preparation for doing their own searches. For the Next step, the children could decide what to ask in the survey and how they will frame the questions, for example, as multiple choice. They could record the results of the survey as a chart.

Find a flight (page 55)
In this activity, the children practise their skills in finding information. They can decide individually what dates and so on to write on the checklist, or the whole class could decide together. Alternatively, you could fill in the details before photocopying. In the Next step, the children could record their results and those of other children on a chart.

House search (page 56)
The children could be given extra criteria for their search, for example, below a certain price limit or in a specific local area. As a further extension, more able pupils can find the location of the house on a map. To practise persuasive writing, they could imagine they are estate agents and write a paragraph about the house, encouraging someone to buy it.

Using keywords (page 57)
You could choose a range of other text extracts from web sites, non-fiction books or CD-ROMs for the children to pick out the keywords. Extend the Next step by allowing the children to try out their keywords and record the web sites they find.

Keyword search (page 58)
Suggest that children write on the chart the first three web sites produced by their search. The chart enables them to evaluate the usefulness of the web sites against the books and CD-ROMs they have used. The sheets can be filed and built up into a valuable classroom resource.

Improve your search (page 59)
This activity is ideal for using with the previous two activities. It encourages the children to anticipate the results that their keywords might produce, and use the refinement of their keywords to rule out any unwanted meanings. The whole class could compare their most useful keywords and discuss why they were useful.

Searching by category (page 60)
Help the children to think about which searching technique might be more appropriate to the kind of information they are trying to find; for example, searching by category can provide a broad overview of a subject, whereas keyword searches may be more useful for finding specific facts.

Web site review (page 61)
You could suggest web sites for the children to review (see pages 88–90 for ideas). They could each review a different web site, then share their opinions with each other and file the completed sheets as a classroom resource for future reference.

What makes a good web site? (page 62)
This page can be used to compare web sites that offer the same kind of information, for example,

news sites. The children can use it to rate the different web sites produced by a search, or you may wish to offer the children a shortlist of web sites to choose from.

For the Internet and Against the Internet (pages 63–64)
Use these pages together to prompt the children to think about advantages and possible drawbacks of using the Internet for research. With younger children, it may be helpful to talk through the ideas first as a class. Children should be aware that the Internet may not always be the best way to find out something. You could list the advantages and disadvantages in a chart and ask the children to compare and contrast the two columns. The activities could form the basis of a class debate on the issue, where the children take a vote on whether they think the Internet is a good or a bad thing.

Points of view (page 65)
This activity helps the children to recognise biased articles and balanced reporting. As a further extension to the activity, they could think about what effect inaccurate reporting might have, both on the reader and on the people involved in the report.

Read all about it! (page 66)
For this activity you will need a collection of old newspapers with printed web addresses (you could ask pupils to bring in old newspapers from home). Instead of listing the key points, the children could print out the web page and underline the key words. They can then base their rewriting of the story on these key words. You could also link this project with the one on page 71. Ask the children to list any words which reveal the writer's point of view.

A poster for book week (page 67)
Pupils can create posters by printing and pasting their text and photographs or, if possible, by importing them into a desktop publishing program. This work could be carried out over a number of lessons.

Time detectives (page 68)
You could suggest that the children print pictures of the people or events and glue them on to the timeline. Remind the children to acknowledge the source of the pictures.

Ancient Egyptian tombs (page 69)
The children can find the tour on Mummies and the Afterlife in ancient Egypt by following the links from the artefact information, or by going to the Tours section of the web site. For the Next step, they could print out a picture of the artefact to accompany their writing.

Finding out about volcanoes (page 70)
For this activity, you may wish to introduce the children to different types of volcanoes, such as cone volcanoes and shield volcanoes. You could also explain some of the different types of volcanic explosions, such as Hawaiian.

Journey into space (page 71)
This activity is based on the NASA web site in the USA. For the Next step, the children could also find facts and pictures for the Sun, the Moon and comets. They could make charts to show the properties of the nine planets, focusing on features such as size or distance from the Sun.

Space Shuttle presentation (page 72)
Before beginning the activity, discuss copyright with the children and explain why it is important to acknowledge the source of any text and pictures they copy directly from the Internet.

From here to there (page 73)
You could provide a printed map or an A–Z of the local area. The children can then print out a map from the Internet and compare how easy it is to read the two versions. Printing maps off the Internet also enables them to draw on routes showing how to get from one place to another. As a further extension activity, the children can read their instructions so that a partner can follow and find the name of the place.

Great inventions (page 74)
The first and third statements are correct; the Internet was invented in 1969. As a further extension activity, the children could put together material for a display on how great inventions of the twentieth century have changed our lives.

Artist profile (page 75)
For this activity, the children will need a selection of books and CD-ROMs containing information about the artists featured. They may need help to understand and extract information from the web sites they visit. You may wish to mask out the names of the artists and insert different ones.

Art review (page 76)
Introduce the activity by discussing how the Internet makes it possible to see exhibits in museums all around the world. You could explain different artistic styles to the children and help them to choose two paintings in the same style. Alternatively, they could do an artist search to try to find two paintings by the same artist. Emphasise to the children that all their views about art are valid as long as they can give evidence in support.

Museums on the web (page 77)
This activity gives the children practice in navigating the web using hyperlinks. You could mask the names of the museums and insert names of ones in your local area. For the Next step, the children may need to refer to maps. Children could display their leaflet for other pupils to read, or e-mail it to children at another school in the area.

The Olympics (page 78)
You could introduce this activity by asking the children what they know about the modern Olympics; for example, how often they take place, where they have recently been held/will soon be held and what sports are played. Encourage the children to find pictures of the Ancient Olympic sports to help them understand how they were played. For the Next step, provide books and CD-ROMs that contain information about sports played at the modern Olympics.

A great day out (page 79)
Start by talking about different kinds of tourist attractions and those the children know in the local area. For the Next step, discuss the sort of things that different people might want to know, including disabled access. The children could choose to target the leaflet at another group of people, such as foreign tourists, and e-mail it to a foreign school. Suggest that the children include reviews in the leaflet from people who have visited the tourist attraction.

Cinema buffs (page 80)
You may wish to introduce the activity by asking the children to bring in adverts for films and then discussing the pictures and the language used. The children should pick a film that they have not seen, to ensure that they extract the information they need from the review. They could hand-draw their posters or import text and pictures into a DTP program.

Celebrity biography (page 81)
Explain to the children what sort of information should be included in a biography, for example, personal details and important events. The children should not write everything they can think of, but should pick out the most interesting facts. You may need to provide them with addresses of search engines to use.

How to make papier-mâché (page 82)
Encourage the children to write the instructions in their own words. As an extension activity, they could look for web sites that explain how to make a papier-mâché animal and continue the instructions as they see necessary.

Going quackers! (page 83)
If necessary, remind the children of the meaning of each of the maths terms on the page. The children are able to choose which set of numbers they want to recognise; encourage them to pick a different set each time they play the game.

League leaders (page 84)
This activity can be done at any point during the football season (August–May). For the extension activity, the children will need squared graph paper.

Sounds of music (page 85)
Introduce the activity by asking whether any of the children play musical instruments and discussing the different ways musical sounds can be made. You could talk about various types of music, such as classical, jazz, blues and so on, and ask the children to think about why certain instruments suit certain types of music. You may need to provide them with addresses of search engines to use.

Joking around (page 86)
Word-play jokes link to word-level work; encourage the children to discuss how the jokes play with word sounds, for example, by using rhyming words or homophones. The children could organise their joke books in chapters (for example, animal jokes, Knock Knock jokes and so on).

Time to celebrate (page 87)
This activity is ideal to use when one of the major festivals is approaching (see the chart below). Before photocopying, write the name of the festival on the sheet. The children could find an e-greetings card on a festivals web site and e-mail it to a friend or relative.

Festival	Religion	Time of year
Holi	Hindu	March
Easter	Christian	March or April
Pesach	Jewish	April
Wesak	Buddhist	May
Rosh Hashanah	Jewish	September
Harvest	Christian	September or October
Divali	Hindu and Sikh	November
Eid-ul-Fitr	Muslim	December
Hanukkah	Jewish	December
Christmas	Christian	December

What's on the Internet?

The Internet is an amazing source of information.

It can tell you tomorrow's weather.

It can tell you about houses for sale.

It can tell you what people wore in ancient Rome.

Write at least two other kinds of information you can find on the Internet. ____________________

____

Where else could you find information about these things?

weather forecast

____

____

houses for sale

____

____

clothes in ancient Rome

____

____

____

Idea bank

telephone directory

shops

More ideas...

Next step

- With a partner or in a group, choose one kind of information.
- Use the Internet and other sources to find the information.
- Discuss why the Internet might be more or less useful than the other sources.

Whom is the Internet for?

The Internet provides information for different people.

Cut out the cards below. On the back of each card, write the purpose of the information and whom it is for. Here's an example.

Welcome to Liverpool FC

Purpose: to provide news and information about the club.

For: fans of Liverpool Football Club.

The Victorian period

By 1894, the average amount of meat consumed by poorer people had risen by 13% (per cent).

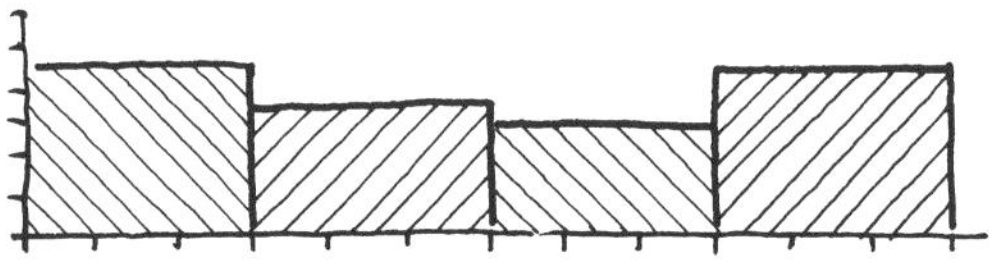

Buy here!

Books
Chart CDs
Top ten videos
Latest game releases

Share prices drop further

Leading shares have fallen to a 12-month low, following profit warnings from major companies.

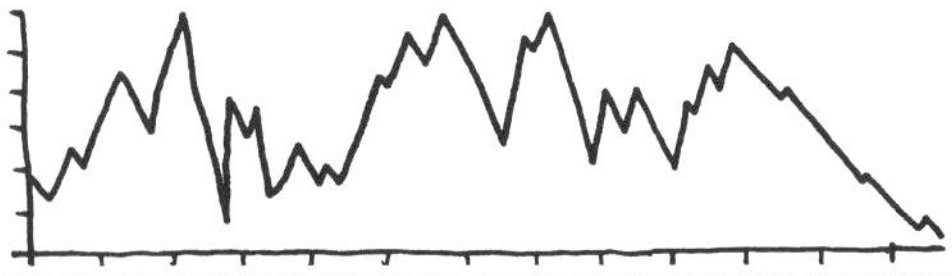

The wolf

A wolf is a wild dog that lives in northern parts of the world. It is a carnivore, which means that it eats meat.

Find out about your family history

Follow five easy steps to start researching your family tree.

Rally driver

Download your free game today!

Next step

- *Carry out a survey to find out what different people use the Internet for. Ask three friends and three adults.*
- *How do they differ? Write a short report.*

Find a flight!

You are going to Disneyland on holiday. You are going to fly with an adult from Heathrow Airport to Orlando, USA.

Here is a checklist of the things you need to decide.

When do you want to go? ____________

When do you want to return? ____________

Do you want to go first class or economy? ____________

Go to one of these web sites.

Circle the one you choose.

www.trailfinders.com   www.britishairways.com   www.thomascook.com

Find flights that match your checklist. Fill in the answers on your ticket.

Name: ______________________________

Number of adults: ____________ Number of children: ____________

Date of departure: ____________

Leaves Heathrow at: ____________ Arrives Orlando at: ____________

Date of return: ____________

Leaves Orlando at: ____________ Arrives Heathrow at: ____________

Price per adult: ____________ Price per child: ____________

First class or economy: ______________________________

Next step

- Compare your results with a friend. Who has the cheapest <u>total</u> fare?
- Work out the difference in the <u>total</u> fare prices. Write your answer here. ____________________

How easy was it to find the information?

Easy ☐

Quite hard ☐

Very hard ☐

House search

You are going to buy a flat or house.

The notepad contains a checklist showing the minimum features you are looking for.

two bedrooms
garden
parking
train station nearby

Go to one of these web sites.

www.berkeleyhomes.co.uk

www.home2view.co.uk

www.excite.co.uk/home

Circle the one you choose.

Find a house in your local area that includes the features on your checklist. Write in the details.

FOR SALE

Type of house ______________________
(for example, detached/bungalow)

Price ______________________

Number of bedrooms ______________________

Garden(s) ______________________

Parking ______________________

Distance from station ______________________

Next step

- Compare your results with a friend.
- Discuss why some houses are more expensive than others.
- Make a list of the features you would most like!

How easy was it to find the information?

Easy	☐
Quite hard	☐
Very hard	☐

Using keywords

To do a search on the Internet, think of important words, or 'keywords', to help you find the information you want.

Read this text. Underline the keywords. (The first one has been done for you.) Write them around the trophy.

The Wimbledon Championships
The Wimbledon Championships are held every year at The All England Croquet and Lawn Tennis Club, in South London. They are generally regarded as the most prestigious of all the Grand Slam tournaments. Top tennis stars come to Wimbledon from all over the world to compete for a place in the final on the famous Centre Court. Members of the Royal family often attend to watch the matches, in particular the Duke and Duchess of Kent, who present the trophies to the champions.

Go to one of these search engines.

Circle the one you choose.

www.askjeeves.co.uk   www.yahoo.co.uk   www.google.com

Type in keywords from the diagram. ____________________

Write the URLs of some web sites you find.

____

____

Find out more about the Wimbledon Championships from the web sites. Write down two more facts.

Next step

- *Think of another sports tournament or event you want to find out about.*
- *Write five keywords you could use.*

Keyword search

I want to find out about ______________________________

I will use these sources of information:

Book 1 ______________________ Author ______________________

Book 2 ______________________ Author ______________________

CD-ROM ______________________

Circle the one you choose.

I will use this search engine:

www.altavista.com www.KidsClick.com www.google.com

Three keywords/phrases I will use are:

1. ______________ 2. ______________ 3. ______________

Search the Internet. Complete the chart.

Sources I used (web site URL/book title/ CD-ROM title)	**How useful?**	**What was most useful about it?**
	0 1 2 3 4 5	
	0 1 2 3 4 5	
	0 1 2 3 4 5	
	0 1 2 3 4 5	
	0 1 2 3 4 5	
	0 1 2 3 4 5	
	0 1 2 3 4 5	

Next step

- Write down anything you found during your search that was completely unexpected.
- Write down any problems you came across when using books, CD-ROMs or the Internet.

Improve your search

I want to find out about ______________________________

____

Circle the one you choose.

I will use this search engine:

www.britannica.com www.yahoo.com www.askjeeves.com

Three keywords/phrases I will use are:

1. ______________ 2. ______________ 3. ______________

Read these tips for improving your search.

Use " " around words that are part of a phrase.
Example: *"stag beetle"*

Use + before words that <u>must</u> appear in the search results.
Example: *beetle+Africa (for African beetles only)*

Use – in front of words that you <u>don't</u> want to appear in the search results.
Example: *beetle–car*

Don't put spaces next to the + or –.

Plan how to improve your keywords.
Redraft them here.

____

____

____

Try out your new keywords using the search engine.

Next step

- *Write the URLs of web sites you find.*
- *Which was the most useful keyword? Can you improve your keywords even further?*

Searching by category

Choose a type of music to find out about, such as classical music.

Type of music: ____________________

I will use this search engine:

Circle the one you choose.

www.bbc.co.uk/cbbc   www.KidsClick.com   www.askjeeves.com

Use the 'search by category' option.
Go to the 'Arts' section.

Follow the links until you find web sites about the type of music you have chosen. Write the links you follow.

Arts →

Write the URLs of the first four web sites you find.

1. ____________________ 3. ____________________

2. ____________________ 4. ____________________

Write three things you find out about the type of music.

1. ____________________

2. ____________________

3. ____________________

Next step

- *Write keywords to help you find out about the same subject.*
- *Do another search using your keywords.*
- *Which search was the most useful? Why?*

Web site review

Use this page to review a web site you have visited.

What I wanted to find out

Name of site

URL

What subjects did the site tell me about?

What else did I find on the site? (pictures/video clips/sounds)

How easy was it to use the site? very difficult 0 1 2 3 4 5 very easy *(Fill in the bar)*

How easy was it to read the text? very difficult 0 1 2 3 4 5 very easy

Was there too much information? too much | just right | not enough

Good things about the site

Not so good things about the site

Overall rating not useful 0 1 2 3 4 5 very useful

Next step

- *Use your notes to write a review of the web site. Remember to give evidence to support your views.*

What makes a good web site?

Visit three web sites which are about the same topic.

The topic is ______________________

Name of site 1: ______________________

URL ______________________

Name of site 2: ______________________

URL ______________________

Name of site 3: ______________________

URL ______________________

You can choose any topic, for example History or Sport.

Rate each site 1 to 5 on the chart.

	Site 1	Site 2	Site 3
Interesting information			
Amount of information			
Easy to understand			
Interesting pictures			
Up-to-date			
Good hyperlinks			
Easy to find what I want			
Looks appealing			

1 = none/not at all

2 = not much/not very

3 = reasonable amount/OK

4 = quite a lot/very

5 = lots/extremely

Most useful thing on each site:

Site 1 ______________________

Site 2 ______________________

Site 3 ______________________

Least useful thing on each site:

Site 1 ______________________

Site 2 ______________________

Site 3 ______________________

Next step

- *Write down other things you think make a good web site.*
- *What do you think are the three most important things?*

For the Internet

These are some of the reasons why people use the Internet for research. Can you think of two more good reasons?

Write your answers in the empty speech bubbles.

Next step

- Carry out a survey to find out what people think is good about using the Internet for research. Ask three friends and three adults.
- Compare the results. Do you think anybody might disagree with their reasons? If so, why?

Against the Internet

These are reasons why some people do not like using the Internet for research.

Can you think of two more reasons against using the Internet? Write your answers in the empty speech bubbles at the bottom of the list.

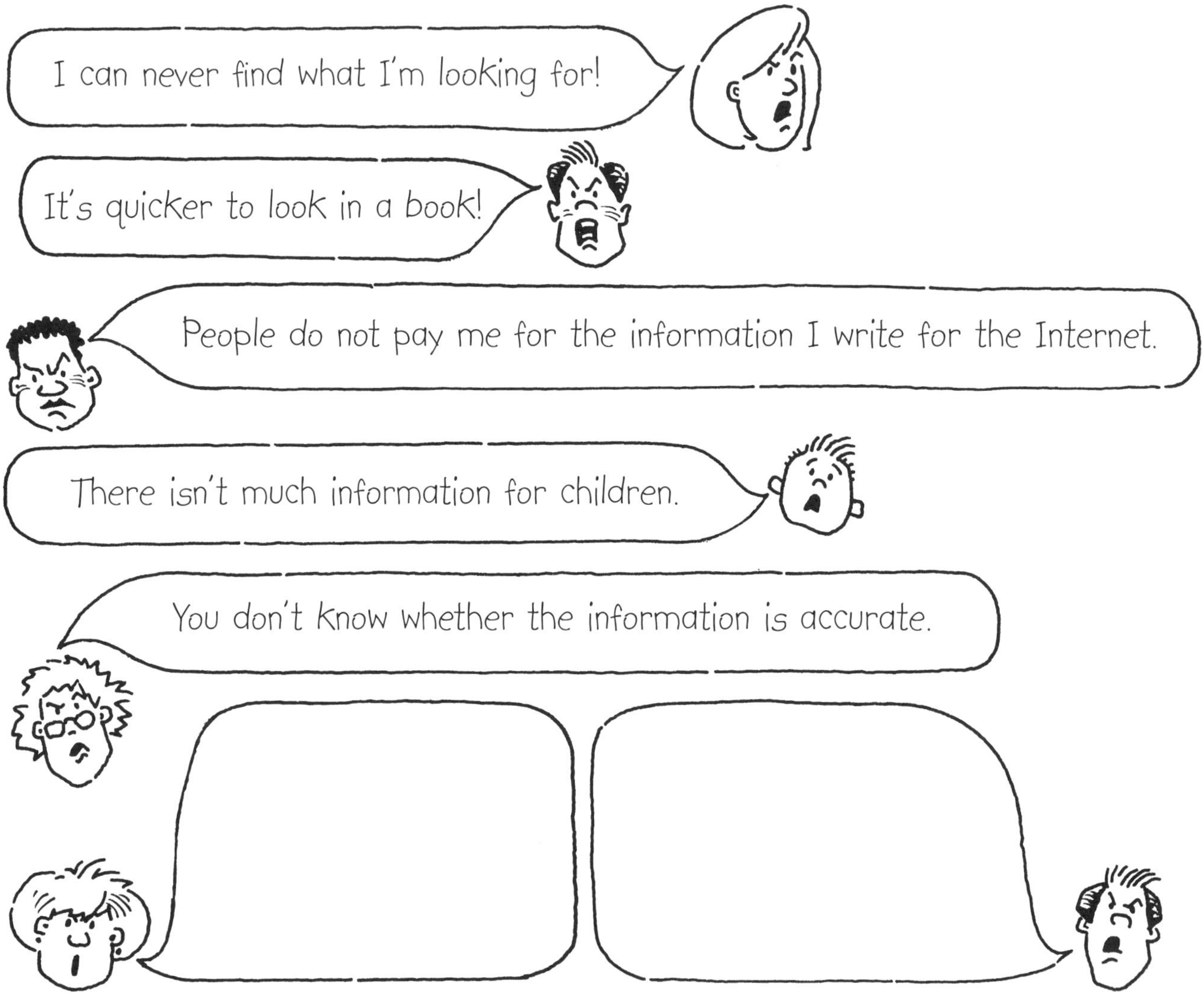

Next step

- Write an argument against using the Internet for research. Use the word bank below.

Word bank

In my opinion	On the other hand ....
Although some people think.............	In conclusion ....

Points of view

Read these two newspaper reports on the same football match.

VICTORY FOR ARSENAL

ARSENAL CELEBRATED a well-earned victory over Manchester United on Saturday. They were in control for most of the match and finally got their reward, scoring superbly from the penalty spot after a nasty tackle from a United defender.

MAN UTD ROBBED

United fans at Saturday's match couldn't believe their eyes when the referee awarded an unjust penalty to Arsenal in the dying seconds.

United had battled bravely and deserved to win the match. But a moment of madness from the referee brought the game to an unhappy end.

Underline the words that show the writer's point of view.

Go to one of these web sites.

Circle the one you choose.

www.timeout.com www.sundaytimes.co.uk http://filmreviews.co.uk

Choose a review of a book, film or sports event.

The title of the review: ____________________

Write words or phrases which tell you about the writer's point of view. ____________________

____

____

Next step

- *Find a news article from a web site or newspaper.*
- *Discuss with a friend how someone with a different point of view might report the same story.*

Read all about it!

Find a newspaper web site address.

Look on the front page of the newspaper.

Name of newspaper: ______________________________

Web site address: ______________________________

Go to the web site.

What is the main news story <u>today</u>? ______________________________

____

What tells you this is the most important story? ______________________________

____

Choose an article from the web site.

Try looking for the keywords to help you.

Headline: ______________________________

List the key points in the article.

1. ______________________________

2. ______________________________

3. ______________________________

4. ______________________________

5. ______________________________

Next step

- *Use your notes to rewrite the story in your own words for the rest of the class.*

How easy was it to find the information?

Easy	☺	
Quite hard	😐	
Very hard	☹	

A poster for book week

My favourite author is ______________________

 Go to a search engine.

www.3.sympatico.ca/alanbrown/kids   www.askjeeves.co.uk

Circle the one you choose.

Enter the author's name, putting the surname first. Write the URLs of web sites which tell you more about the author.

____

____

____

Write four more facts you find out from the web sites.

1. ______________________

2. ______________________

3. ______________________

4. ______________________

Create a folder on your hard disk. Give it the author's name. Type your notes as a report and save it in your folder. Download a photograph of the author. Save it in your folder.

Next step

- *Use the information to create a poster about your author.*

Time detectives

Look at this Tudor timeline.

Go to one of these history web sites.

Circle the one you choose.

www.bbc.co.uk/history/timelines www.tudorhistory.org

Can you find the missing names and dates from the web site? Write them in the spaces. Write some other important events on the timeline.

1485 ← ________________ becomes king. He is the first Tudor monarch.

[ ] ← Henry VIII becomes king.

[ ] ← Edward VI becomes king, aged nine.

1558 ← ________________ becomes queen. She was the last Tudor monarch.

1580 ← Sir ________________ sails round the world.

[ ] ← James I becomes king.

Next step

- *Word-process your timeline for a classroom display. If possible, find pictures from the Internet and paste them in your document.*

How easy was it to find the information?

Easy	☐
Quite hard	☐
Very hard	☐

Ancient Egyptian tombs

Go to the British Museum web site.

www.thebritishmuseum.ac.uk/compass

Enter keywords to search for the ancient Egyptian objects shown below. Write the clue number in the circle next to the correct picture. Write the name of the object.

Clue 1: This object was made for a woman called Satdjehuty. It tells us that she was very wealthy and important.

Clue 2: This object is almost entirely covered with gold leaf. It shows a Theban priestess called Henutmehyt.

Clue 3: This object came from the tomb of a man called Merymose. He was very wealthy and had three coffins made out of stone.

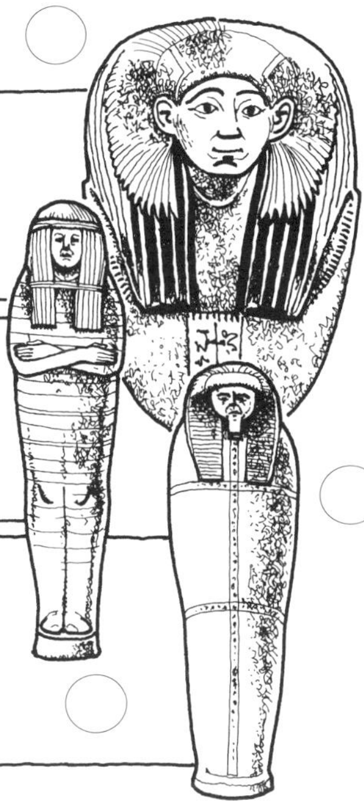

Name: ____________________

Name: ____________________

Name: ____________________

Find and join the **tour** called 'Mummies and the Afterlife in ancient Egypt'. Then answer these questions.

Why did the ancient Egyptians mummify bodies? ____________________

What was the purpose of the outer stone sarcophagus? ____________________

What were Books of the Dead for? ____________________

Next step

- *Find another object from ancient Egypt on the British Museum web site.*
- *Write about it in your own words.*

How easy was it to find the information?

Easy	☺	☐
Quite hard	😐	☐
Very hard	☹	☐

Finding out about volcanoes

Choose one of these volcanoes.

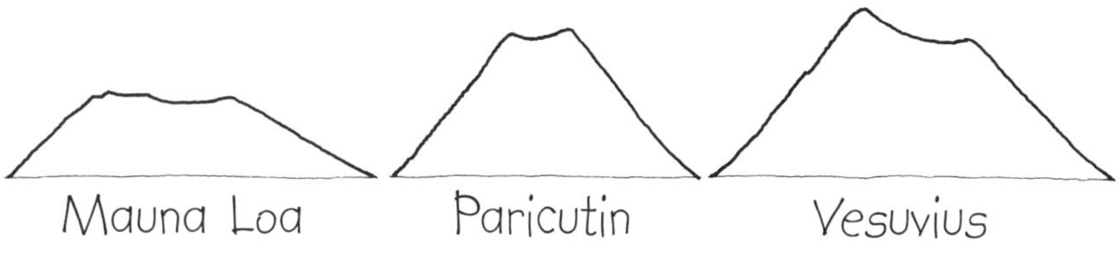

Circle the one you choose.

Go to one of these web sites.

http://vulcan.wr.usgs/gov   www.yahoo.com   http://volcano.und.nodak.edu

Find out about your volcano and complete the fact file. Then use the information you find to help you number the diagram.

Name of volcano: __________

Continent: __________

Active or dormant? __________

Height: __________

The most recent eruption was in __________

Three more facts:

1. __________

2. __________

3. __________

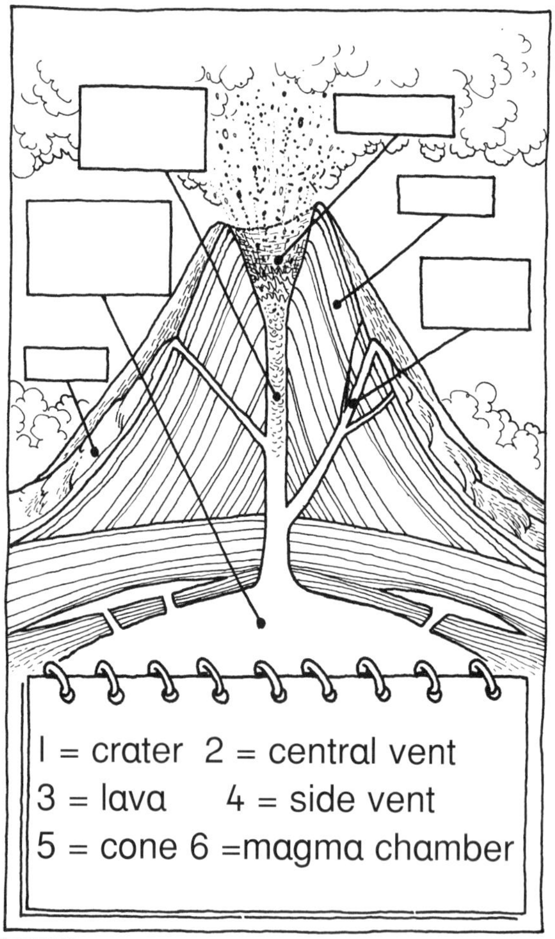

Next step

- *Compare your fact file with a friend who has researched a different volcano.*
- *Make a chart to show similarities and differences.*

Mauna Loa and Vesuvius	
Similarities	Differences

How easy was it to find the information?

Easy	☺	
Quite hard	😐	
Very hard	☹	

Journey into space

Go to http://kids.msfc.nasa.gov/SolarSystem/

Find **Space Kids: Solar System Tour**. Click on the icon.

Explore the site and the hyperlinks. Look for information about planets in our Solar System. Write a fact about each planet.

Planet ____________
Fact ____________

Planet ____________
Fact ____________

Planet ____________
Fact ____________

Planet ____________
Fact ____________

Planet ____________
Fact ____________

Planet ____________
Fact ____________

Planet ____________
Fact ____________

Planet ____________
Fact ____________

Planet ____________
Fact ____________

Next step

- Find real photographs of the planets on the Space Kids web pages. Download them.
- Word-process your planet facts. Paste the photographs alongside the text.

How easy was it to find the information?

Easy ☐
Quite hard ☐
Very hard ☐

Space Shuttle presentation

Use this page to make notes for a presentation on the Space Shuttle.

Create a new folder on your hard disk.

Name your folder 'Space Shuttle presentation'.

 Go to http://www.nasa.gov

Find the **NASA for Kids** icon. Click on it.

Use the web pages to help you answer these questions.

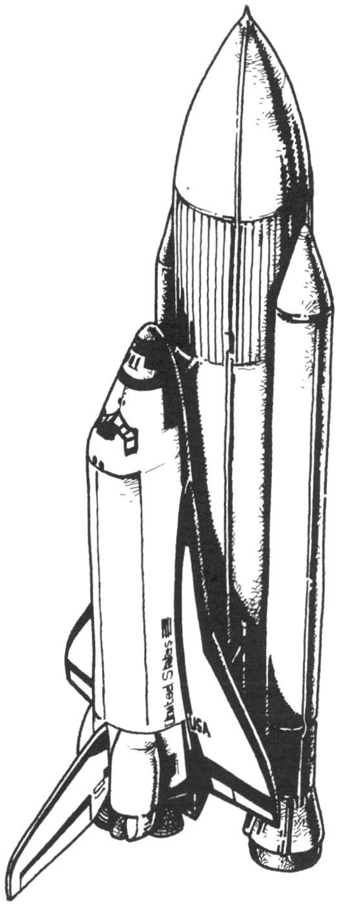

What does a Space Shuttle do?

___

How many Space Shuttles does NASA have?

___

What are their names?

___

___

___

___

What are the four main parts of a Space Shuttle?

___ ___

___ ___

What does each part do?

___ ___

___ ___

Find a picture of a Space Shuttle. Copy it into your folder. Now word-process your notes and save them in your folder.

Next step

- *Edit your pictures and text for a class presentation.*
- *Acknowledge the source of your material.*
- *Print out your presentation.*

How easy was it to find the information?

Easy	☺
Quite hard	😐
Very hard	☹

From here to there

Write the name of the road you live on and your postcode.

Circle the one you choose.

Go to one of these web sites.

www.mapquest.co.uk   www.streetmap.co.uk

Enter your road name or postcode to find a map of where you live.

Find your road on the map. Then find a place near your home. Write the name of the place.

The place can be a train station, a park or a main road.

Imagine you want to tell a friend how to get from your home to the place you have chosen. Write instructions.

(Example) Turn right out of the gate. Walk to the end of the road. Turn left on to Trinity Street . . .

Next step

- Choose one of these streets: Vulcan Street in Aberystwyth or Graham Close in Scarborough.
- Enter the name of the street on the web site.
- Write instructions for getting from there to the seaside.

How easy was it to find the information?

Easy	☐
Quite hard	☐
Very hard	☐

Great inventions

Go to one of these web sites.

Circle the one you choose.

www.scienceweb.org.uk   www.bbc.co.uk   www.yahooligans.com

Use the web site to find out about the history of computers. Tick whether each statement is true or false.

In the 1830s, Charles Babbage invented a calculator that could remember numbers.	true	☐	false	☐
The Internet was invented in 1987.	true	☐	false	☐
In 1946, US engineers built the first electronic digital computer.	true	☐	false	☐

Find out three things that modern computers can do.

1. ____________________
2. ____________________
3. ____________________

Idea bank

Car design

E-mail

How did people do these things before computers were invented? Find out from the web site.

____

____

____

Next step

- Think of another important invention, such as television or the space satellite.
- Find out when it was invented and why it is important. Write down what you find out. List the sources you use.

Use books, CD-ROMs or web sites.

How easy was it to find the information?

Easy ☐

Quite hard ☐

Very hard ☐

Artist profile

Choose one of these artists, or think of a different one.

Monet

Constable

Van Gogh

Find out about the artist. Write your notes here.

Use books and CD-ROMs.

Full name: ______________________

Date of birth: ______________________

Where lived: ______________________

Famous paintings: ______________________

Museums where you can see them: ______________________

____

Do a search to find pictures by your artist. Use the artist's name, his paintings and the museums as keywords.

Bookmark the best web sites you find.

Download a picture that the artist painted.

Name of painting: ______________________

What I like/don't like about it: ______________________

____

Next step

- Word-process an artist profile using your notes. Add any more information you have found.
- Paste in the picture.

How easy was it to find the information?

Easy	☺	☐
Quite hard	😐	☐
Very hard	☹	☐

Art review

Go to the web site for the New York Museum of Modern Art. www.moma.com

Find a painting that you like.

Title: ________________ Artist: ________________ When painted: ________

Now go to the web site of the Tate Modern in London.

Find another painting that you like.

It could be by the same artist or in a similar style.

Title: ________________ Artist : ________________ When painted: ________

Complete the chart.

	Painting 1 (Moma)	Painting 2 (Tate Modern)
What is the painting of?		
What words describe the atmosphere? (Does it make you feel happy, warm, peaceful . . .?)		
Why do you like the painting?		

Next step

- Create a folder on your hard disk and call it **Art review**.
- Download the pictures and save them in your folder.
- Word-process a report comparing the two paintings. Paste in the pictures.

Museums on the web

Go to http://www.mda.org.uk/vlmp

Find these museums.

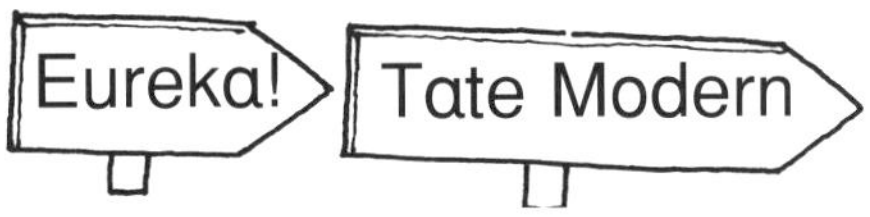

Follow the links to their web sites. Complete the charts.

Eureka!

Web site URL: ____________________

Town/city: ____________________

The museum has displays about

____

____

____

Three things to see or do:

____

____

____

I would/would not like to visit this museum because...

____

____

____

Tate Modern

Web site URL: ____________________

Town/city: ____________________

The museum has displays about

____

____

____

Three things to see or do:

____

____

____

I would/would not like to visit this museum because...

____

____

Next step

- Go back to http://www.mda.org.uk/vlmp. Find out about a museum near your home.
- With your group, make a leaflet for other pupils called 'Our Local Museums'. Write about what you think other children will find interesting.

How easy was it to find the information?

Easy	☺	☐
Quite hard	😐	☐
Very hard	☹	☐

The Olympics

The Ancient Olympics took place between 776 BC and AD 394 in Olympia, Greece. Like the modern Olympics, they were held every four years.

Go to www.olympics.com or www.perseus.tufts.edu/Olympics

Find out how each of these sports at the Ancient Olympics was played.

Sport	How it was played
Chariot racing	
Riding	
Boxing	
Pankration	
Pentathlon (five events)	
Event 1	
Event 2	
Event 3	
Event 4	
Event 5	

Next step

- Find out whether any of the sports are still played at the modern Olympics.
- Draw another chart showing some of the sports that are played today and how they are played.

Use books, CD-ROMs or web sites.

How easy was it to find the information?

Easy	☺	☐
Quite hard	😐	☐
Very hard	☹	☐

A great day out

Go to the Tourist Information web site
www.official-touristboards.co.uk

It might be a theme park or a historic place.

Find a tourist attraction close to where you live.
Complete the information on the poster.

Name of attraction ______________________

Location ______________________

Opening times ______________________

Entry price ______________________

Five things to do ______________________

____

____

____

____

____

How to get there by public transport ______________________

____

How to get there by road ______________________

____

Telephone number ______________________

Web site ______________________

Write what town it is in or near, and the county.

Include days of the week and times.

Is it different for adults and children?

Write in your own words.

Which is your favourite?

Where is the nearest train or bus station?

Give directions.

Next step

- *Discuss with your group which parts of the attraction might be interesting to families.*
- *Create a leaflet for the attraction aimed at families.*

How easy was it to find the information?

Easy	☺	
Quite hard	😐	
Very hard	☹	

Cinema buffs

Go to one of these search engines.

www.disney.co.uk   www.warnervillage.co.uk

Circle the one you choose.

Go to the **Entertainment** section. Find a web site that tells you what films are on at the cinema this week.

Web site URL: ______________________________

Choose a U or PG certificate film you would like to see. ______________________________

Find a review of the film. Write about it on the clapperboard.

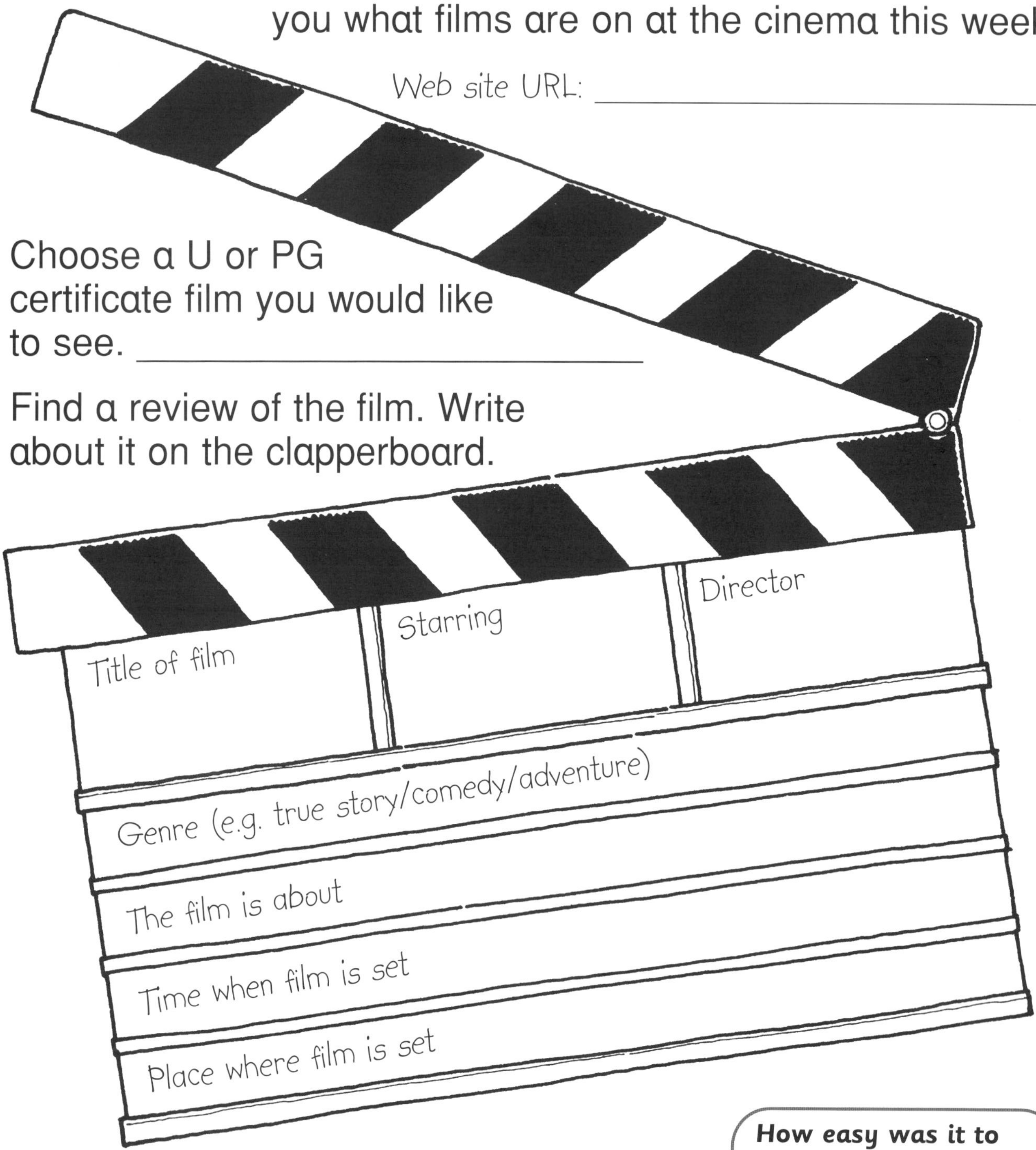

Next step

- Create a poster for the film using what you have found out. Make up a slogan and add quotes from the review. Draw a picture that shows what the film is about.

How easy was it to find the information?

Easy	☺	☐
Quite hard	😐	☐
Very hard	☹	☐

Celebrity biography

A biography tells the story of someone else's life.

Write the name of a famous person.
Fill in the things you already know about him or her.

Name: ______________________________

Age: ______________________________

Family details: ______________________________

Where lives: ______________________________

Job: ______________________________

Why famous: ______________________________

Hobbies: ______________________________

Achievements: ______________________________

____

____

Do a search on the Internet to find out more.
Use words from your notes as keywords.

Keyword list	Useful web sites

Next step

- *Use your notes to write a biography of the celebrity. Find a photograph to include, from a magazine or from the Internet.*

How easy was it to find the information?

Easy	☐
Quite hard	☐
Very hard	☐

How to make papier-mâché

Go to one of these search engines.

www.eduweb.co.uk   www.goto.com

Circle the one you choose.

Do a search to find a web site that tells you how to make papier-mâché.

Keywords: ______________________________

Web site URL: ______________________________

Write the instructions in your own words.

Word bank

First
Then
Next
Finally

Ingredients

1. ______________________________
____
____

2. ______________________________
____

3. ______________________________
____

4. ______________________________
____

5. ______________________________

Next step

- Find out how to play a board game, such as backgammon or dominoes.
- Write a sentence about the aim of the game. Try to explain how to play in five steps.

Use books, CD-ROMs or web sites.

How easy was it to find the information?

Easy ☐
Quite hard ☐
Very hard ☐

Going quackers!

You need to have your wits about you for this maths game! First, write ten of each type of number on each duck.

Now go to http:// www.mathsyear2000.org.

Find the **Mallard Maths** game. Read the instructions, then start playing!

Record your scores here.

Game 1	Game 2	Game 3
Game 4	Game 5	Game 6

Next step

- *Play another game on the Maths Year 2000 web site.*
- *Draw a chart to record your scores.*

League leaders

Go to one of these search engines.

www.lycos.co.uk www.yahoo.com

Circle the one you choose.

Go to the **Sports** section. Find a web site showing the Premier League table.

Web site URL: ____________________

Record the information on this chart.

Position	Team	Games played	Points
1st			
2nd			
3rd			
4th			
5th			

Each team gets 3 points for a win, 1 point for a draw and 0 points for a loss.

Help **Fanatical Fergus** to fill in the gaps.
Show your workings on a separate piece of paper.

1. The team in fifth position is _____ points behind the top team.

2. This season, each team will play a total of 38 league matches. There are _____ games left to be played.

3. If the top team wins all its remaining matches, it will finish the season with _____ points.

4. If the team in fourth position wins half its remaining matches and draws half, it will finish the season with _____ points.

Next step

- *On a piece of graph paper, produce a graph showing the positions of the top five teams.*

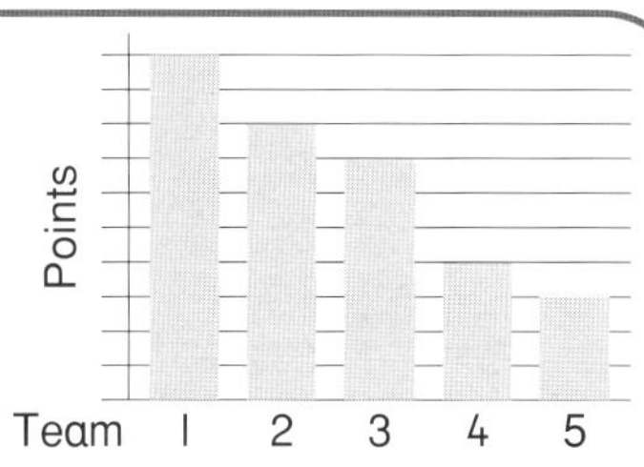

How easy was it to find the information?

Easy	☺	☐
Quite hard	😐	☐
Very hard	☹	☐

Sounds of music

Choose a musical instrument. You could pick one of these, or choose another.

Write down anything you already know about the instrument.

Instrument: ______________________

Made of: ______________________

____

A word that describes the sound the instrument makes: ______________________

Who invented it? When and where? ______________________

Types of music often played on the instrument: ______________________

Famous musicians who played the instrument: ______________________

____

Other facts: ______________________

____

Go to a search engine. Look in the **Music** section to find web sites which tell you more. Add to or correct your notes.

Bookmark the best web sites you find.

Find a sound file of your instrument being played. Then find out how the sound is made.

Next step

- *Create a folder on your hard disk. Give it the name of your instrument. Download the sound file into your folder.*
- *Word-process your notes as an encyclopedia entry. Save it in your folder.*

How easy was it to find the information?

Easy	☺	☐
Quite hard	😐	☐
Very hard	☹	☐

Joking around

What kind of dessert can you find in a forest?
Chocolate moose!

This joke plays on words which sound the same: *moose* and *mousse*.

Search the Internet to find some more jokes that use words which sound the same. Write them on the book pages below.

I will use this search engine: ____________________

Three keywords I will use are: 1. ____________________

2. ____________________ 3. ____________________

Useful web site URLs are: 1. ____________________

2. ____________________

Next step

- With your group, put together a joke book. Illustrate the jokes.
- Design a cover for your book.

How easy was it to find the information?

Easy ☐

Quite hard ☐

Very hard ☐

Time to celebrate

Write down anything you already know about this festival.

Festival: ______________________

Religion: ______________________

Time of year (spring/summer/autumn/winter): ______________________

What the festival celebrates: ______________________

Ways people celebrate: ______________________

Useful web site URLs: ______________________

Go to one of these web sites to find out more. Correct your notes and write more things you find out below.

Circle the one you choose.

www.standards.dfee.gov.uk/schemes/religion
www.namess.org.uk/fests.htm
www.svtc.org.uk/rme/websites/themes/festivals.asp

Follow hyperlinks to other web sites and bookmark the useful ones.

Next step

- Find pictures showing how the festival is celebrated and download them.
- Use the pictures as ideas for a greetings card. If possible, print out a picture and glue it on to your card.

How easy was it to find the information?

Easy ☺	☐
Quite hard 😐	☐
Very hard ☹	☐

Section 5: RECOMMENDED WEB SITES

In this section you will find addresses of recommended web sites the authors have used personally and in training sessions with teachers. Each URL is for a web site's home page. You may have to click a further link or more to find exactly what you want.

The web sites are grouped into categories. A brief description is given of the content of a typical web site in each category.

HINTS AND TIPS

If the Internet is very busy, you may hit a 'traffic jam'. A web site may go off-line briefly to be updated.

Look in educational magazines and newspaper supplements for more useful web site recommendations.

Category	Type	URL	Notes
Books			
These sites provide the basis for reading lists, learning about authors and book publishing.			
	The Book Trust	www.booktrust.org.uk	
	Children's Literature	www.acs.ucalgary.ca	
	Scottish Book Trust	www.scottishbooktrust.com	
Downloads			
If your school service provider does not regularly upgrade your software, here are the web sites from which you can download upgrades at no cost.			
	Internet Explorer®	www.microsoft.com/windows	Browsers upgrades and add-ons
	Netscape®	www.netscape.com	The other main browser
	Shareware	www.shareware.com	Links to other download sites
Educational			
Useful sites for general use of computers in the classroom.			
	Beginner's Centre	www.northernwebs.com/bc	A user's guide to the Internet
	Eduweb/Learning Alive	www.learningalive.co.uk	Research Machine's portal site
	Microsoft	www.microsoft.com/education	In and Out the Classroom links
	Becta	www.becta.org.uk/index.html	
Experts			
	Pitsco	www.askanexpert.com	Where children can 'ask the expert'
Government strategies, curricula and qualifications			
Official sites for details of the national curriculum, schemes of work and standards.			
	Curriculum 2000	www.curriculum2000.co.uk	Curriculum 2000 for UK schools
	DfEE	www.dfee.gov.uk	Department of Education
	National Curriculum	www.nc.uk.net	National Curriculum online
	Standards	www.standards.dfee.gov.uk	Literacy/Numeracy/Schemes
	VTC – England	www.vtc.ngfl.gov.uk	Virtual Teachers Centre: England
	VTC – Scotland VTC	www.svtc.org.uk	Virtual Teachers Centre: Scotland
	VTC – Cymru	www.vtccymru.ngfl.wales.gov.uk	Virtual Teachers Centre: Wales
IAP			
	Information on . . .	www.thedirectory.org	Addresses of access providers

Museums

A selection of sites that allow you to view collections of works of art, historical items and natural history. Some of the sites allow you to tour the museum, and many of them provide excellent reference material you can download.

British Museum	www.thebritishmuseum.ac.uk	The British Museum, London
Centre Pompidou	www.centre.pompidou.fr	Centre Pompidou, Paris
Hermitage	www.hermitagemuseum.org	State Museum, St Petersburg
Imperial War	www.iwm.org.uk	Links to other wartime life sites
Metropolitan	www.metmuseum.org	Metropolitan Museum of New York
MoMI	www.bfi.org.uk	Museum of the Moving Image
Musée d'Orsay	www.musee-orsay.fr	Musée d'Orsay, Paris
Natural History	www.nhm.ac.uk	London's fabulous museum
NMPFT	www.nmpft.org.uk	National Museum of Photography, Film & TV
National Gallery	www.nationalgallery.org.uk	The National Gallery, London
National Railway	www.nrm.org.uk	National Railway Museum
Natural History	www.ology.amnh.org	US site with dinosaur activities
Science Museum	www.nmsi.ac.uk	Gateway to other museum sites
The Tate Museum	www.tate.org.uk	Links to other sites – Tate Modern

Newspapers

The Guardian	www.guardian.co.uk	UK newspaper
Independent	www.independent.co.uk	UK newspaper
New York Times	www.nytimes.com	US newspaper
Washington Post	www.washingtonpost.com	US newspaper

Parents

These sites offer additional resources that you may need for special downloads (plug-ins) to function properly.

DfEE Parents Centre	www.parents.dfee.gov.uk	Information and links
Schoolzone	www.schoolzone.co.uk	Information and links

Plug-ins

Quicktime™	www.apple.com	Used to play video clips
RealPlayer®	www.real.com	For on-line stores and radio stations
Shockwave®	www.macromedia.com	To display 'Flash' animations
	www.timecast.com	Real Audio sites and live concerts

Qualifications

Sites offering educational resources.

OCR	www.ocr.org.uk	Oxford, Cambridge & RSA

Reference and Resources

Aesop's Fables	www.umass.edu/aesop/contents.html	Texts to download and use
Ancient Egypt	www.ancientegypt.co.uk/home/html	Information about Ancient Egypt
Dorling Kindersley	www.dk.com	CD-ROMs and books
Encarta	www.encarta.msn.com	Packed with multimedia
Oxford ED	www.oed.com	Standard Oxford Dictionary
PastPix	www.pastpix.com	Pictures to simulate
Primary Resources	www.primaryresources.co.uk	Classroom resources
Project Gutenberg	http://promo.net	Free downloads of classic texts
Teacher Resource Enchange	www.contribute.ngfl.gov.uk	Exchange of teachers' work
Wacky Web Tales	www.eduplace.com/tales/index.html	Fun stories for classroom use

Safety issues

Superhighway Safety	www.epals.com	
	www.safety.ngfl.gov.uk	
	www.safekids.com	

Science

NASA homepage	www.nasa.gov	Earth and space science resources
The Meteorological Office	www.met-office.gov.uk/education/	Weather reports, maps, information
Yorkshire Electricity	www.yeg.co.uk/fun/	All about electricity for children

Search Engines

Directories and indexes for starting keyword searches.

Alta Vista®	www.altavista.com	
AskJeeves™	www.ask.com	Question-based
Ask Jeeves for kids	www.ajkids.com	Question-based kids search
Excite	www.excite.co.uk	Uk-based general search
Google®	www.google.com	
HotBot®	www.hotbot.com	
Lycos®	www.lycos.com	
Magellan	www.magellan.excite.com	Popular web Directory
Mirago	www.mirago.co.uk	Uk-based general search
UK Plus	www.ukplus.co.uk	Uk-based general search
Yahoo UK/Ireland®	www.yahoo.co.uk	Uk-based general search
Yahooligans	www.yahooligans.com	Yahoo's kids search

Software

Web sites from where software can be downloaded.

Becta Software	www.besd.becta.org.uk	
Compression	www.winzip.com	Winzip® for Windows
General	www.download.com	
Shared	www.shareware.com	Software on a shared basis
Softease	www.textease.com	DTP, Database, Spreadsheet package

Special Needs

These sites offer advice and resources for SEN.

DfEE ICT support	www.dfee.gov.uk/sen	SEN links etc.
NASEN	www.nasen.org.uk	National Association for Special Educational Needs
BDA	www.bda-dyslexia.org.uk	British Dyslexia Association
RNIB	www.rnib.org.uk	Royal National Institute for the Blind
NAGC	www.rmplc.co.uk/orgs/nagc	National Association for Gifted Children

Teachers

Web sites offering a range of cross-curricular ideas and resources.

AskJeeves for . . .	www.ajschools.com/teachers	Useful resources & ideas
BBC Education	www.bbc.co.uk/education/schools	Home page with numerous links
Click Teaching	www.clickteaching.com	Useful resources and ideas
Educate the Children	www.educate.org.uk/teacher_zone	Useful ideas and information
EPals	www.epals.com	Classroom exchanges by e-mail
ICTteachers	www.icteachers.co.uk/	Useful resources and ideas
ICT toolbox	http://crduk.extra.bt.com/ict/toolbox	BTs school resources site
Kent LEA	www.kented.org.uk/ngfl	LEA site with ideas and resources
Northern Grid	www.northerngrid.org	Northern LEA Consortium
Schoolzone	www.schoolzone.co.uk	Ideas & Information for teachers and parents
School Express	www.freeworksheets.com	American site with free worksheets
Spot Pages	www.freenetpages.co.uk	Key Stage1 resources and ideas
Stockport LEA	www.stockportmbc.gov.uk	LEA site with ideas and resources
Sunshine Online	www.literacyhour.co.uk/index.html	Simple ideas for lessons
Teacher Net	www.teachernet.gov.uk	
Teaching Ideas	www.teachingideas.co.uk	Ideas and resources including ICT
VTC – England	www.timeplan.com	Virtual Teachers Centre – England
VTC – Scotland	www.svtc.org.uk	Virtual Teachers Centre – Scotland
VTC – Cymru	www.vtccymru.ngfl.wales.gov.uk	Virtual Teachers Centre – Wales
Welcome to the web	www.teachingideas.co.uk	Excellent Internet activities

TV news

BBC	www.bbc.co.uk	Home page with numerous links
ITN	www.itn.co.uk	British network
CNN	www.cnn.com	American network
Virgin Radio	www. virginradio.co.uk	

Section 6: AT-A-GLANCE GUIDES

This section contains a basic checklist of computer skills and an explanation of jargon words used in this book. You may find it useful to make copies of pages 91 to 93 for posting in the classroom, computer room or at home.

What basic skills do I need?

Your PC	☐	Turn on and start up the computer
	☐	Know your way around the keyboard
	☐	Load and use a CD-ROM
	☐	Turn on and set up a printer
Mouse Skills	☐	Use a mouse to select icons
	☐	Use a mouse to drag and drop objects
	☐	Use a mouse to open and close windows
	☐	Single-click and double-click to open applications (programs)
The Task Bar	☐	Find the task bar on the desktop
	☐	Use the task bar to run more than one program and switch between programs
	☐	Click on the system tray on the task bar
The Start Button	☐	Click on the *Start* button on the task bar to open the *Start* menu
	☐	Launch programs from the *Start* menu
	☐	Use the *Start* menu to shut down
Desktop Icons	☐	Double-click on an icon to start a program
	☐	Drag and drop icons around the desktop and rearrange them to tidy the desktop
	☐	Double-click on an icon to open another window
Desktop Windows	☐	Move a window by dragging on the title bar
	☐	Use the *Close* button
	☐	Use the *Minimise* and *Restore* buttons
	☐	Restore a window from the task bar
Disks, Folders, Files	☐	Name and save a file on to the hard drive
	☐	Transfer work from a floppy disk
	☐	Choose a file from a folder

USING THIS CHART

Here we have listed the skills needed to use computers efficiently and confidently in the classroom or at home. Go through the list, ticking each item if you know it or as you learn it.

You may also want to photocopy these pages and use them as a record of your pupils progress.

Disks, Folders, Files (continued)	☐	Create and name a folder
	☐	Click on a drive to see the files and folders
	☐	Save work in appropriately named files
	☐	Retrieve saved files from folders
	☐	Add, change and re-save a file
Information Backup	☐	Establish a routine of backing up work
	☐	Copy files on to floppy disks
	☐	Store back-up disks in a safe place
My Computer	☐	Find the *My Computer* icon
	☐	Double-click on the *My Computer* icon to look at the drives
	☐	Double-click to look at the *Control Panel*
	☐	Close the *My Computer* window
The Recycle Bin	☐	Delete an old work file in the *My Computer* window
	☐	Double-click on the *Recycle Bin* to see what is stored there temporarily
	☐	Restore a file held in the *Recycle Bin*
	☐	Permanently delete a file
Control Panel	☐	Find and launch the *Control Panel* window from the *Start* menu
	☐	Select the mouse icon in the *Control Panel* to change its speed
	☐	Close the *Control Panel* window
Printers	☐	Check the printer is on and ready to use
	☐	Use the *Print Preview* option
	☐	Use the *Quick Print* button
	☐	Print out more than one copy using the *Print* dialogue boxes
	☐	Choose one page from a longer document to print out
The Internet	☐	Log on to the Internet
	☐	Visit web site by entering its address
	☐	Bookmark a web site to explore later
	☐	Send an e-mail
	☐	Read an e-mail from your Inbox
	☐	Store an e-mail address in the Address Book
	☐	Log off from the Internet

It Pays to Practise:

- Mouse skills such as clicking and dragging
- Navigating the desktop and knowing where to find:
  - ▲ the floppy disk drive
  - ▲ CD-ROM drive
  - ▲ *My Computer*
  - ▲ *My Documents*
  - ▲ *My Briefcase*
  - ▲ the *Recycle Bin*
  - ▲ the applications
- Handling windows:
  - ▲ dragging
  - ▲ resizing/minimising
  - ▲ scrolling
  - ▲ closing down
- Routine 'housekeeping' – creating a useful filing system with folders and files organised systematically
- Saving across a network and backing up files as a regular precaution
- Loading a printer with paper, clearing paper jams and changing ink cartridges
- Becoming familiar with the accepted terms for screen features, actions and resources.

GLOSSARY

access provider A company that lets you connect to the Internet by dialling into their computer. *See also* Internet Service Provider.

address On the Internet, the precise location of a particular web site or web page, which is also known as its URL. *See also* URL.

ADSL Short for 'asymmetric digital subscriber line'. A high-speed permanent connection to the Internet. *See also* ISDN.

animated GIF Two or more image files combined to create a very simple moving picture or animation. *See also* GIF.

application A software program designed to let you do particular kinds of task on your computer. A word-processing application, for example, is designed for working onscreen with words but no pictures.

back-ups Copies of computer files kept on storage disks, not your hard disk. It is vital to make and keep back-ups in case files are lost or corrupted. *See also* floppy disk.

bandwidth Measures the amount of information that can be transferred over an Internet telephone connection.

bin An area on your hard disk where deleted files stay until a decision is made to get rid of them. On an Apple Macintosh computer the bin is called the Wastebasket.

bookmarks *Netscape Navigator*'s way of storing direct links to the addresses of favourite web sites. *See also* 'Favorites'.

browser The vital piece of Internet software for viewing pages from the World Wide Web. The two most popular browsers are *Internet Explorer* and *Netscape Navigator*.

cache A folder on your hard drive in which your browser stores all the files it downloads from the World Wide Web (in case you want to view those pages again).

CD-ROM Short for 'compact disc, read only memory'. Used for games, information and software installation, this sort of compact disc cannot be recorded over (hence 'read-only').

clip art Images that have been created by someone else for you to use on computer.

clipboard An area on your hard disk where anything you copy or cut from a file is temporarily stored until it is pasted into another file (or another place in the same file).

cookie A small text file that some web sites store on your computer so that they know who you are next time you visit.

copy, cut, paste A set of really useful editing tools found within many kinds of programs including word processors and browsers.

copyright Laws that protect text and images from unlawful copying.

cyberspace A word coined by William Gibson in his novel *Necromancer*. It is used as a very generalised term for the Internet and everything that comes with it.

Data Protection Act Act of law designed to protect individuals from misuse of information held on computer or file about them. Find out more about it from: **http://www.open.gov.uk/dpr/dprhome.htm.**

database A collection of stored records which might include text, images and/or numbers.

digital camera A camera that does not use photographic film that needs processing, but instead captures and stores images as digital files. These files can be transferred on to your computer for display, printing out, sending in an e-mail attachment, or posting on a web page.

domain name The unique name given to every web site on the Internet such as: **www.sitetraining.com**

download To copy computer data from one computer to another (or to a disk), possibly via the Internet. The opposite term is uploading.

drag, drop Moving icons, text or objects around onscreen. To drag something, click the mouse button over it and move the mouse with the button held down. Drop the object in the right place by releasing the mouse button.

DTP Short for 'desktop publishing'. Describes applications that combine word-processing functions with image-handling functions.

export To send data from one computer program to another. For example, you can export an image that you have found on the Internet in a format that you could use in a DTP program.

FAQ Short for 'frequently asked questions'. These – along with their answers – are often displayed on a web site or in a newsgroup.

favorites A menu in Microsoft's *Internet Explorer* browser (and a corresponding folder on your hard disk) that contains short-cuts to web sites that you visit regularly. *See also* Bookmarks.

file format The type of file. For example, a JPEG is a file format that is suitable for images, whereas Text Only is one format suitable for words.

file management Organising your computer files according to a sensible, user-friendly system. This is especially important when the use of a computer is shared.

floppy disk A storage device on which you can back up small files (usually up to 1.44 Mb). Despite its name, a floppy disk is square and hard – the round, floppy bit is hidden inside.

font A style of lettering, for example **bold,** *italic* or roman.

freeware Software that you do not have to pay for.

gateway A program or device that acts as a kind of translator between two networks so that they can communicate with each other.

GIF Short for 'graphic interchange format'. One of the two most common file formats for graphics used on the Internet. *See also* JPEG.

graphics General term describing images created and stored on computers.

graphing program A program that will create charts and graphs from the data entered.

history list A list stored by your browser showing recently visited web sites so that you can see where you have been and revisit sites easily.

home page (1) The page displayed by your browser when you start it up, or when you click the *Home* button. (2) The first page (or main contents page) of a web site.

host A computer connected directly to the Internet, usually all the time, such as your Internet Service Provider's computer. The host machine allows other computers to connect to it.

housekeeping Regular computer system maintenance such as deleting out-of-date files, organising files into directories or folders, making back-up copies of files and emptying the Recycle Bin.

HTML Short for 'hypertext mark-up language'. The computer code used to create web pages and links.

http Short for 'hypertext transport protocol'. Often forms the beginning of a web site address or URL.

icon A small picture onscreen that represents a function, program, file or folder. You can click on an icon to jump to a different place or to perform a task.

ICT Short for 'Information and Communication Technology', now one of the core subjects of the National Curriculum.

image map A single image divided into several 'hot' areas and placed on a web page. Each area will take you to a different page or file when clicked.

import To receive some computer data from another program or storage device.

Internet A huge network of computers, all linked together and able to exchange information, that no one completely owns or controls. Sometimes, its name is shortened to 'the Net'.

Internet Explorer The name of Microsoft's browser software. *See also* Browser.

Internet Service or Access Provider (ISP/ISA) A company that allows you to connect to the Internet by dialling into their host machine. *See also* host.

Intranet A network of computers that are linked together using Internet technology, but are private and not accessible to everyone. Many educational institutions have an Intranet.

ISDN Short for 'integrated services digital network'. A kind of telephone line that can handle (transport) lots of complex data, including large images, very speedily.

JPEG Short for 'joint photographic experts group'. One of the two most common file formats for images used on the Internet. *See also* GIF.

keyword, key phrase A word or phrase that you type into a search engine, so that it can look for any web sites that may contain information relevant to that word or phrase.

log off To disconnect from the Internet, so that your browser breaks the link with the host computer.

log on To connect to the Internet, by telling your browser to dial up and form a link with the host computer. Often, you have to identify yourself at the start of a session, by typing in a username and password. *See also* username.

menu The list of possible options in a program.

mirror site An exact copy of a web site, located on a different computer.

modem A device that allows a computer to send and receive digital information down analogue phone lines. It may be inside or outside the computer.

multimedia A mix of differently formatted information, for example text, still images, sound files and animation, such as is stored on a CD-ROM.

netiquette Term used to describe accepted rules of behaviour on the Internet (formed from 'Net' and 'etiquette'). An example of bad netiquette is typing e-mails in capital letters, which looks like you are shouting.

network Two or more computers that are connected to each other by cables, or that can be connected to each other via modems and telephone lines, so that they can swap data.

newsgroup A group of Internet users that swap ideas and opinions on a shared, common interest.

offline Not connected to the Internet but able to continue working on files. *See also* online.

online Connected to the Internet. *See also* offline.

portal An Internet site that has a search engine and a directory of links to other web sites. Portals make good starting points for Internet searches.

QCA Short for 'Qualifications and Curriculum Authority'.

qwerty Describes the traditional keyboard arrangement, as on a typewriter's keys: the letters 'q', 'w', 'e', 'r', 't' and 'y' are the first letter keys to appear at the top left.

RAM Short for 'random access memory'. Short-term memory used by your computer.

refresh, reload Forcing the browser to download a web page again by clicking a tool bar button labelled *Refresh* (in *Internet Explorer*) or *Reload* (in *Netscape Navigator*). This can be useful if the page seems to have 'frozen'.

ROM Short for 'read-only memory'. A way of storing information so that it can be read very fast, but not changed in any way, for example on a CD-ROM. *See also* CD-ROM.

search engine A web site that maintains an index of other web pages and sites, allowing you to search for pages on a particular subject by entering keywords or key phrases. Examples include *Yahoo* and *Google*.

server A computer that provides a service, such as hosting many web sites or connecting to your service provider's mail server when you decide to send or receive e-mail.

service provider A company that gives you access to the Internet by letting you dial in to their computer. This may be an Internet Service Provider or an online service.

URL Short for 'uniform resource locator'. The unique address of a web site or web page.

username The unique name that you use when using your computer in order to identify yourself.

virus A piece of computer code that can attach itself to programs or files on your computer and corrupt or delete them. To avoid 'catching' a virus, check any new files you download using anti-virus software.

WAP Short for 'wireless application protocol'. Describes web-like pages written in a language called WML (similar to HTML) that can be downloaded into WAP-enabled mobile phones and pagers.

web page A single document (usually with **.htm** or **.html** at the end of its name) that is a tiny part of the Internet. Web pages may contain text, images and links to other web pages.

web server A computer or program dedicated to storing Web pages and transmitting them to your computer, to be viewed in your browser.

web site A collection of related web pages and files, usually created by or belonging to a single individual or company, and located on the same web server.

word bank A list of words, phrases and pictures that children can click on, rather than typing in the words for themselves. Word banks can be created in some educational software, such as *Textease*, and cut down on errors due to mispellings.

word processor A computer program that allows the user to input text and edit it.

World Wide Web A vast collection of documents and files stored on web servers. The documents are known as web pages and are created using a language called HTML. All these pages and files are linked together by a common language called hypertext.

www Short for 'World Wide Web'. Often found at the beginning of a web address or URL.

INDEX

Printed and bound in Great Britain